Perseus
The Warrior of Peace

Translated from French by Gilad Sommer.
Edited by Gilad Sommer, Harianto Mehta, Sangeeta Iyer.
Re-designed for English edition by Janki Shah, Neha Mehta.
Published in 2018 by

NEW ACROPOLIS

New Acropolis Cultural Organization.
Mumbai, India.
www.acropolis.org.in
info@acropolis.org.in

ISBN: 978-81-920193-5-2

Printed in India.

Perseus
The Warrior of Peace

Fernand Schwarz

Table of Contents

FOREWORD

I met Fernand Schwarz in 1979, in Paris, France, where he teaches the daily practice of Philosophy, and he quickly became my philosophy master. In 1986 I left for Israel, and it has now already been more than 30 years since I left. But paradoxically, this distance has brought me closer to him and his teachings, which I consider to be an everyday practice.

When Fernand Schwarz writes, he relies on his own experiences. In this book he reveals the keys which enable every person to awaken the latent hero that lies within. It is a path he himself has tread, giving this book a powerful authenticity rarely seen today. As he explains in the book, we must first free ourselves in order to try and liberate others.

Fernand Schwarz is a man who will often say just the right words to push someone out of their entrenchments; a bit like a modern Socrates. It is not an easy task to be his disciple, for he forces movement, adaptation and the letting go of the shelter of preconceptions and acquired habits. He shows us that by diminishing our comfort zones we become capable of building inner change. He encourages this evolution through the strength of his convictions and his own personal example.

Without this change, this book would be but another collection of ideas; undoubtedly interesting, but nothing more. However, this work contains hidden opportunities, concepts that appear in the middle of a sentence, half-buried in a paragraph, which are true treasures for those who know to recognize them.

Among other things, Fernand Schwarz writes, "the Path of our own evolution exists only when we set out." He explains that when an individual enters the heroic path, he draws out abilities he did not suspect he had! The key to our destiny always lies within us, here and now, although it is often easier to imagine that we will find it elsewhere.

Do not be mistaken. This is not a psychology textbook that teaches how to "live better". This book is a polished mirror - like the shield from Athena that was offered to Perseus - in which the reader can see himself, or herself, more objectively.

The author explains that we should not be afraid to assert our destiny. That is where the hero is. He urges us to awaken that hero.

Fernand Schwarz is no longer a Warrior of Peace; he is a Warrior of Wisdom. He has arrived at the third and final stage of the course he teaches; he is the Philosopher-turned-Politician, who returns to the Cave of Plato to enlighten those who are still chained.

He is a philosopher because Love, that tireless motor that always pushes us to face new challenges, guides him in his timeless quest for Wisdom.

He is a Politician who, unlike in the modern sense of the word, is a visionary who proposes a valid, real and applicable solution to the chaos of our times. He proposes a renewal of the human being so that civilization can be reborn from the ashes of barbarity.

He is a Warrior of Wisdom. He offers only what he has experienced and mastered himself. You can only really offer what you are.

Fernand Schwarz is my master, and although I strive for objectivity when speaking of him, I know for a fact that from this exercise I shall not emerge victorious. I can only urge the readers to judge for themselves, by walking the path in their turn and making it their own. To set oneself in motion is, as Fernand Schwarz writes, the only way to awaken the hero that is sleeping within oneself, and accept one's destiny.

Pierre Poulain

I dedicate this book to Thierry, Fred, and Mica, without whom the quest for Perseus would never have been possible.

Note of Thanks to Dan Millman

I would also like to thank Dan Millman, who I have never actually met. Several years ago, however, when I was asked to organize youth activities, someone recommended his book *Way of the Peaceful Warrior.*[1]

I was very surprised by the thoughts and teachings that Dan Millman expressed in his book. They were very familiar concepts that, although I had learned about them in a completely different way, resonated with me in a very profound way.

"To really help people, you first need to understand them – but first understand yourself, prepare yourself; develop the clarity, the courage, and the sensitivity to exert the right leverage, in the right place, at the right time. Then your actions will have power."[2]

"Someday, you will write, teach, and do other things, too, to reach out to your spiritual family, to remind them of their mission, to give the clarion call."[3]

"The secret of change is to focus all your energy not on fighting the old, but on building the new."[4]

---

1 *Way of the Peaceful Warrior: A Book that Changes Lives*, Dan Millman, HJ Kramer, 2006
2 *The Sacred Journey of the Peaceful Warrior*, Dan Millman, HJ Kramer, 2004
3 Ibid.
4 *Way of the Peaceful Warrior: A Book that Changes Lives*, Dan Millman, HJ Kramer, 2006

PREFACE: A SHORT HISTORY

I was born in the middle of the last century. My father taught me at a very early age where money comes from, and I learned that I owed it to the very large number of workers and craftsmen who worked in his textile factory. At six, my father took me to work with him, so that I could understand what life was about. Every year during my summer vacation, I learned a new trade. In truth, I didn't want to, but I followed his directions, motivated by respect and a sense of fidelity.

I got to know all the people in that beehive, who were busy transforming threads into fabrics and clothes. Each took his job seriously but a good mood reigned. My father was probably there for some reason. What is certain is that everyone curiously observed me - the child who was to learn from them, who was asking many questions, imagining himself a professional already. I also asked them about their lives; where they came from, about their motivations. All, at one time or another, expressed some suffering, but also the joy of accomplishing their tasks. Each had had his own inner struggle. For them, fighting in life was not a question of violence, but of dignity.

With that and my studies, at about the same age, I began practicing martial arts and Greco-Roman wrestling. It so happened that three of my mother's brothers were sports champions. The eldest brother had returned from Japan in the mid-1950s. He was one of the few Argentinians to have been admitted into a Japanese dojo, returning to Argentina with a 3rd dan black belt in Judo. To make a living, he established the first Judo dojo in the capital. One day he came home and asked my mother if he could take me to the dojo. My mother looked at my father and they both agreed. As I was a restless child, they imagined that such an activity would calm me down a little. I did not know where I was to be taken. My uncle had presented to me a small kimono, and suddenly I found myself with other children and teenagers, practicing warm-up exercises. Then we moved on to combat sessions, *randori* in Japanese. To my surprise, I saw my uncle approach me, inviting me to fight. I was really very surprised. He showed me how to wear the kimono. Everything progressed from that point on. I was repeatedly flying through the air and falling, not knowing when it would end. Curiously, I was not worried. Some instinct told me not to resist, and to go with the flow. At one point, everything stopped. We bowed; the fight was over. I found myself in the midst of a crowd of practitioners, unable to understand what had just happened to me.

When I returned, I asked my uncle why he was interested in fighting me. After a while he asked me if I was afraid of falling. I said no, noting that I had not gotten hurt and that I had gotten back up every time I fell. "That is your first lesson," he replied.

In combat, the first thing to learn is how to fall (*uke* in Japanese), to get up, to recover, and not to be afraid. The first battle is the fight against ourselves. The key is to keep moving. To do so, resistance is not the most important thing; we must allow things to run their course by adapting. This teaching had a great impact on me: let go of your pride in order to win.

Months of learning to fall followed, falling in every way possible, and of course, learning to get up. I also learned to observe my opponents and infer what they can teach me, and to adapt to their way of fighting.

As a teenager, I became an activist in order to protect my community from anti-Semitic injustice and violence. My friends and I were unafraid to fight extremists, who sometimes attacked schools or synagogues. I thought that because we had a just ideal, we could allow ourselves to act violently for a noble cause.

But the unexpected happened. Under my father's instruction I had to learn the business of banking. Upon mentioning that one of my passions was ancient philosophy, a secretary informed me that in Buenos Aires there was a school of philosophy at which she was enrolled. I was very surprised. I asked her many questions about this school and I too registered. There I met my master. I already knew about Plato and Aristotle, but I did not know much about Eastern philosophy. The encounter with a true master of philosophy was a shock…

My childhood memories of the inner struggle resurfaced, out of nowhere.

The year that followed was a turning point. Through the teachings of my master, I understood that we had to find a solution for all mankind and not just for a particular collective or community, because basically we are all the same, and we belong to one humanity. Victory could not be achieved by violence. It was necessary to find other means - inner victory. To become a peaceful warrior. To promote civilization, not barbarism.

"The smallest step we make inside of ourselves towards the

good is, in a way, a step made by all of mankind. No individual is without historical responsibility, but no one is master and lord of history. [...] If every day you triumph in yourself over a bad tendency; If every year you rule a vice; If every decade you can improve your self-control, you are making history, and you are not only helping yourself but all other human beings through your action."[5]

My journey had just begun...

In 2010, thinking about the difficulties faced by today's young people in finding themselves and especially in believing in their future, I reflected on how one might help them build adequate tools to face the challenges of our times.

Convinced that they have no way to make their voices heard, or to find their place, young people today can be compared to dying whales who strand themselves on a beach.

Many no longer believe in themselves. No help, credit or external contribution, no technical measure no matter how laudable, will be of effect if we fail to awaken the ability to dream. An old adage says that one must "dare, know, be able, act". Young people lack the ability of imagining themselves differently. They lack the pioneers' zeal to dream of a new world, a new continent, yet to be explored - not external, as in the case of America, but internal - the cradle of the human being.

The teachings that I received a long time ago, and which I now pass forward are, above all, intended for the youth. These teachings can be summed up in what others later called "the quest for the peaceful warrior."

---

5 Jorge Livraga, Italian Philosopher, born in Buenos Aires, author of numerous books and founder of the international association New Acropolis. This is taken from a conference he gave in 1980 called *What is the meaning of being a human being?*

The ideal of the warrior, or the peaceful warrior, is not a new concept; it has existed since time immemorial. Despite the violence and the great difficulties that human beings have gone through, driven by the ease and mechanics of instincts, and prone to dominating others, and to the subjugation or destruction of others, there has always been, since the earliest traditions, philosophers, men and women, sometimes barely known, who decided to act otherwise, choosing the path of the peaceful warrior. For millennia, in all civilizations, men, women, and groups, have chosen to live in accordance with the model of the peaceful warrior. Naturally, human beings are more prone to violence, impulsiveness, anger, and hatred. But it is surprising, and also comforting at the same time, that this very old lineage of people, despite never having met, have grasped and have wanted to live a common model, one in which the real struggle is within oneself.

It is a long history and, contrary to what we have often learned in school, for hundreds of thousands of years, man has maintained relationships of mutual assistance. While natural selection has played its part, so have solidarity, exchange and the need to help others.

The most interesting civilizations, past and present, have developed solidarity - in addition to a process of selection and qualification - as an essential aspect in the successful realization of a human society, i.e. individuals who can count on each other!

I understood that it was necessary to start from the beginning; that is to say, to give meaning, not in an intellectual way but through daily action, and to appeal to young people who wanted to be in contact with their soul, the higher dimension of their being, and transmit this quest to their peers. To do this, I relied on three disciples with whom I shared several adventures, and this allowed me to put a small group of young people to the test, through their own questioning, and to discover the depth of their souls, in order to build the future.

The quest of Perseus was born from all these experiences that I had lived and shared.[6]

I am deeply grateful to the hundreds of young people who, through their experiences, questions and challenges, allowed me to adapt the old teachings I had received into a new form, giving rise to the theory and practice of the peaceful warrior.

6 Perseus, a hero of Greek Mythology, son of Zeus and Danae. His Myth influenced Christian legends, especially that of St. Michael and the dragon.

CHAPTER I

Choosing Between Egoism and Altruism

"Everybody knows egoism exists, but when we recognize that altruism is inherent to human nature, we have made a great step towards the advent of a culture of opening up towards the other." - *Matthieu Ricard*

New generations, all over the world, are moved by a deep desire for an authenticity they cannot find in contemporary societies. A personal philosophical investigation is necessary to rediscover the conditions for lasting happiness at the individual and collective levels. Our consumer societies have proven that they cannot provide good answers. Faced with the confusion caused by fears and doubts, the choice between selfishness and altruism emerges as a major issue. For our societies to become more human, a different culture and way of life are necessary; one which takes into account our inner aptitudes for harmony. Our education, however, and especially the mental images that have been transmitted to us, seems to be a major obstacle.

For the last two centuries, our societies, inspired by the idea that man is fundamentally selfish, have encouraged models of competition based on the idea of the survival of the fittest.

Biologist Richard Dawkins[7] popularized the idea that genes are selfish by nature, suggesting that individuals therefore must be as well. But one does not necessarily imply the other, and Dawkins was perplexed by this problem.

By observing the altruistic behavior of animals, such as the case of a small monkey in a zoological garden protecting its keeper from a large furious baboon, Darwin concluded that natural selection, which promotes selfish instincts, also promotes the evolution of altruism. A gene seeks to reproduce, and its success can potentially ensure a never-ending life. On the other hand, natural selection can steer a network of genes that forms an organism and imposes a form of altruism that can go as far as the sacrifice of its own reproductive faculties, or even its own life, because the laws of life will always favor the integrity of the whole over the needs of a part. This can be seen clearly in the case of white blood cells that renounce their own existence for the good of the organism.

We find the same laws that govern the infinitely small, at work within the framework of the evolution of species. Contrary to what one might imagine, selfish individuals are not the greatest victors of evolution. According to a certain logic, one would think that natural selection would eliminate the overly generous individual. In 2006, however, Vincent Jansen, a scientist from the University of London, together with Minus Van Baalen, a member of the CNRS, used mathematical modeling to show that altruistic animals manage to retain an advantage, since altruists recognize each other and together manage to thwart the traps of selfish individuals seeking to profit from a certain situation.

7 British biologist and ethnologist (born 1941), evolutionary theorist who wrote *The Selfish Gene*, Oxford University Press, 1976.

It was this intuition that led Charles Darwin[8], in "La Lignee humaine," to observe that altruistic behavior is not reserved for close relatives: "Great civilized men, who have never before risked their life for anyone, have overcome their instinct of self-preservation and dove into a torrent to save a drowning man, even if he was a stranger."[9] In this he joins the Chinese philosopher Mencius[10] who wrote: "Every human being, without exception, when seeing a child fall into a well, immediately experiences a strong feeling of distress."

Altruism does not only have cultural roots. It is part of the laws of nature. Unfortunately, we only retained the theory of the evolution of species, the idea of the survival of the fittest, and the struggle of one against the other, whereas reality is much more nuanced. According to the latest scientific research, selfishness and blind violence are not the best strategies for preserving species and their evolution.

In his book "Altruism," Matthieu Ricard, a Buddhist monk and disciple of the Dalai Lama, tells us that new scientific discoveries made in the last thirty years have demonstrated that true altruism exists and can be applied beyond our close relationships, towards our fellow humans and non-humans.

Collaborations between neuro-scientists and meditators have shown that with training, altruism and compassion are qualities that can be cultivated.

Studies have shown that the practice of altruism and compassion unquestionably brings about functional and structural changes in our brain and could even change the

---

8 English naturalist (1809-1882) whose work on the evolution of living species revolutionized biology with his book "*On the Origin of Species by Means of Natural Selection, or the Preservation of Favoured Races in the Struggle for Life*", published in 1859.

9 *Altruism*, Matthieu Richard, Brown and Company, 2015, 864 pgs.

10 Chinese Confucian thinker (380 - 289 BC) in search of a sage-king capable of restoring peace and author of The Mencius, one of the Four Books forming the Five Classics, the neo-Confucian corpus as defined by Zhu Xi, great reformer of the Song Dynasty.

expression of our genes. These studies have also made it possible to differentiate between empathy (the ability to enter into a state of affective resonance with the other), altruism (wishing that the other is happy) and compassion (the desire for the other to be free from suffering).

Although competition is generally more visible and dramatic than cooperation, recent work has shown that cooperation has played a much greater role in the course of evolution, and in the creation of increasing levels of complexity and organization.

In his book, Matthieu Ricard reflects on the mental state that leads to altruism. The practice of empathy alone is not enough to generate altruism.[11] The importance of the open display of compassion to all suffering beings is highlighted by psychologists, neuro-scientists and Buddhists; it occupies a central place in altruism. With compassion, the human being is aware of the situation of others, wants to relieve their suffering and obtain their well-being. The individual is not drained by confusion between one's own emotions and those of others.[12] It is not necessary to feel the suffering of the other as in the case of empathy.[13]

Altruistic love creates a positive space within us that serves as an antidote to empathetic distress, and prevents emotional resonance from amplifying to the point of becoming paralyzing and from engendering the emotional exhaustion which is characteristic of burn-out. Without love and compassion, empathy by itself is like an electric pump in which water no longer circulates.[14]

---

11 *Altruism*, Matthieu Richard, Brown and Company, 2015, 864 pgs.
12 Ibid
13 Ibid
14 Ibid

The theses of Felix Warneken[15] and Michael Tomasello[16] demonstrate the existence of altruistic tendencies in the early stages of human ontogeny and testify to the natural disposition to altruism. In fact, we are biologically programmed for restricted altruism, but this capacity can serve as a basis for extended altruism, which is true human altruism, in which the individual desires the good of others, or rather of the community.

This leads some individuals to take on significant risks that might threaten their own survival; it is only then that we can truly speak of altruism in the strict sense. When speaking of the human being, more than instinct, one must speak of dispositions towards altruism and towards selfishness. What we are is not only determined by our genes, but also by our experience, our culture and our education, which guide us to use our natural dispositions in one direction or another.

Denis Peter[17] points out that we have moved away from the type of social relationships which motivate our altruistic dispositions. Hence, at present they are underdeveloped or rendered ineffective in maintaining a minimum degree of harmony and well-being. For example, the need for recognition, now associated with a competitive and individualistic lifestyle, has increased competition and ill-being at the expense of altruism.

One may wonder whether human evolution has favored individualists or altruists. The latest studies show us that it has favored altruists, but the give-and-take between the individual and the group remains a field in perpetual evolution.

---

15 Associate professor of Social Sciences, Department of Psychology, Harvard University, who studies the emotional nature and cooperation of young children and chimpanzees.

16 American psychologist (born 1950) co-director of the Max Plank Institute of evolutionary anthropology. Researches the cognitive abilities of human beings and great apes, author of *The Cultural Origins of Human Cognition*, Harvard University Press, 1999, 256 pages, and *Why We Cooperate*, MIT Press, 2009. 232 pgs.

17 Altruisme et évolution, http://humanismepur.free.fr/ethique/altruisme_evolution.php

Cultural Altruism, a Necessary Condition for Evolution

Human altruism is more ancient than we may think. As an anthropologist, I have always been fascinated by the early manifestations of altruism in different human societies, all the way to the very beginnings of humanity. "One can create a good life in two ways," explains Christopher Boehm,[18] "The first is to punish evil and the second is to actively promote virtue."

Boehm presents both in his theory of social selection. Altruism can be defined as a form of extra-familial generosity, as opposed to nepotism, which concerns only relatives. For Boehm, the need for human altruism emerges clearly in the study of the moral guidelines of hunter-gatherer societies.

Aided by a research assistant, he compiled thousands of pages of accounts of anthropologists who have studied the hundred and fifty hunter-gatherer societies in the world today. This observation highlighted the importance of cooperation and solidarity for the evolution of a human group.

Our current models of competition and selection are a break from this ancient model; they are continuing to get worse, making us become more and more specialized instead of fueling a broader perspective. This position makes us more vulnerable because it imprisons us, preventing us from hearing anything that does not express the dominant worldview, making it impossible for new forms of action to emerge. In fact, creative adaptation is inhibited by such a stand. This results in confinement and withdrawal, a form of petrification and stiffness, a rigidity that invades our human societies, an alarming sign of aging.

18 An American cultural anthropologist who studies human behavior and great primates (conflict resolution, altruism...), author of *Moral Origins: Social Selection and the Evolution of Virtue, Altruism, and Shame*. New York: Basic Books.

David Lordkipanidze, director of the excavation team at the Dmanisi site in Georgia, came to a very important conclusion: human beings were already caring for their elders 1.8 million years ago. This discovery was made by studying a hominid skull, Homo Georgicus, who had a brain only half the size of ours. His jaw had only one canine tooth, he had lost his other teeth very early. Despite the resulting difficulties in feeding, especially with meat, the main source of nourishment at the time, he had managed to live till the age of 45, that is to say, the age of elders in his community. It is clear that in order to survive, the group had to take care of him, which means that others chewed his food.

This implies an early existence of a complex social organization which made the choice between selfishness and altruism - to care for the sick and the elderly. And this was long before the appearance of the current Homo Sapiens. But Lordkipanidze is not alone. Alejandro Bonmati, a lead researcher of the Atapuerca site, located near the city of Burgos in Spain, says the same thing. About ten years ago, the skeleton of an elderly man was found at the excavation site, with serious lesions on his back, which would have caused him to walk bent over, and move about with great difficulty. It is clear that he had had this deformity from an early age, and that he could not have hunted or aided the group's survival. He was obliged to receive the help of his peers in order to move and eat.

Altruism and egalitarianism are systems that promote individual freedom. Respecting these moral rules prevents a person from taking advantage of others, or from dominating a whole group using unjust privileges.[19] Altruistic love or extended altruism thus makes it possible to dissolve egocentrism. Choosing altruism not only benefits others, but also oneself, as a means to become nobler, to become better.

---

19 Blog run by Eric-Michael Johnson: http://blogs.scientificamerican.com/primate-diaries.

Altruistic love dissolves the seeds of violence that are within us. The need to withdraw from violence by understanding others and by rejecting instinctive forms was an important part of my master's teachings. He said: "The important thing is that mankind will rise above ignorance, cruelty and selfishness, and it doesn't matter who the people leading it are, provided that no one is left behind. The seeds of hatred flourish in disaster; action always engenders reaction. Do not be violent and, sooner or later, violence will cease."[20]

Psychiatry today shows us that the worst criminals have experienced great suffering. Crime is a way of escaping their own suffering by making others suffer. On a smaller scale, this is like the temptation we may have to avenge our own suffering by causing pain. This is inconsistent with the path of the peaceful warrior because violence is a transgression of its rules.

When we slowly begin to cultivate violent reactions, we become accustomed to acting violently, and we transgress the rules or boundaries. We do not realize it when this transgression takes place. As with drugs, one becomes accustomed to the feeling of power, the rise of adrenaline that diverts inner power. When we get used to the adrenaline, we discern less and less the boundaries we cross, or the taboos we transgress.

Materialistic society has created an enormous convergence of social violence, and is unable to manage itself without producing more violence. We should not be surprised at what is happening to us. However, anyone that wants to engage with a path of self-transformation cannot take part in this behavior pattern.

20 *Take flight*, Jorge A. Livraga, Ed. NA, 2002, page 38.

CHAPTER II

The Art of Mastering Oneself by Adaptation

A phrase from Tao Te Ching by Lao Tse inspired me in defining the path of the peaceful warrior. "Softness triumphs over hardness and strength. Flexibility surpasses rigidity. These are the principles that inspire us to control things by following their course, the art of mastery by adaptation."

It has always amazed me that life for the Egyptians in the times of the pyramids was thought of as a journey of sailing between the horizons of birth and death, the waters of the Nile representing life itself. An interesting thing about sailing is that we cannot brake with a single stroke; it is impossible, we will always drift. Performing any maneuver while sailing requires us to learn to cruise by following the current, the wind, the counter-currents and a thousand other jests of the elements. One learns to control, as the phrase of Lao Tse says, by following the course of things. To oppose or to resist is impossible and is not even very intelligent. To adapt, while keeping on course, is necessary.

Our western education, in wishing to control and subdue everything, tries to classify and fix everything to a specific place, making things immobile. We tend to freeze things, to view them as static entities, having the sad delusional belief that they will never move, and will always be available to us where we left them.

One day, while playing chess, my master told me, "How lucky we are to play this game, where we have the luxury of playing on an immobile checkerboard." In life, the squares change color and the pieces transform. In reality, nothing is static and everything transforms, to the great displeasure of those who wish to control everything.

Why do we want to control everything, failing to take life into consideration? Because we are afraid of life and the changes it brings. A part of us always wants to be reassured, to fix things in place so that everything will always stay the same, thus demanding minimum energy and effort. We think it is a way of preserving ourselves, of gaining on death.

But this strategy in life makes us mechanical, insensitive to change and evolution. For sure, we are alive, but the deepest part of us remains inert, as if it were dead. We realize many actions, and feel ourselves to be alive, but we remain unconscious, not drawing from experience, not changing. This reminds me of Plato's Myth of the Cave, where a large number of people are chained to their seats, and are watching the shadows that reflect what is happening outside the cave, projected on the back wall of the cave. They spend all their time discussing these shadows, without having any idea of what they really are, believing that they know, and have mastered the situation.

To understand the truth, we must free ourselves from our chains, stand up and go outside to face the sunlight and the unknown environment. But our inner comfort zone is so important to us, and so highly encouraged by our society, that it is hard to decide to take action. This comfort zone is not just about physical comforts, but also includes psychological and intellectual comforts. How many times do we refuse to hear things, or think of things, because they disturb us and challenge our beliefs, or our convictions? Such situations require us to make an effort on ourselves, to surpass ourselves, and to transform ourselves.

It is by diminishing our comfort zone that we are able to build inner change, to take Lao Tse's proposal as our own.

Warrior of Peace: Is This a Contradiction?

The notions of a warrior and of peace seem to be irreconcilably contradictory. And in our epoch, we do not like contradictions. We do not know how to handle them. We are taught to put things into two columns: correct and incorrect. This is called formal logic, wherein the principle of exclusion applies, and is very reassuring. Something is either white or black, hot or cold, a man or a woman, day or night, good or evil. Thus when you place yourself on one side, you see from a certain vantage point those who are on the other side. From there it will seem that the fault, the responsibility for what is wrong, is never yours - but lies with those who are on the other side.

Paradoxically, this binary vision, which is very useful for our technology and for the development of a spoken and written language, is not capable of rendering reality. It can only facilitate a fragmented vision. And we desperately stand by the fragments that suit us in order to reassure ourselves. For example, what time is it on the planet? With the binary approach, the answer would be the time at the place at which we currently are. But in reality our dear planet Earth lives all twenty-four hours simultaneously. And as per binary logic, such a concept is unthinkable. "Is it day or night on planet Earth?" The answer is: both. Everything happens at the same time.

To understand this, we must think day **and** night, man **and** woman, hot **and** cold. It is the logic of inclusion, which integrates the parts into a vital global whole. It is by this alone that we can practice the art of uniting the opposites, a principle which supports life, and which lies at the very heart of the teachings of my master and of my own approach.

We must be warriors in order to fight our indifference, our selfishness, our separateness, our fragmented vision and our pettiness. The warrior in question is not a bloody killer but is engaged in the battle within oneself.

The peaceful person is not the person who wishes to be left alone in peace, who does nothing that may disturb him or cause himself to be noticed. The peaceful person is the person who can live in peace with his conscience, the source of calmness and serenity which helps us face the difficulties of life. The peaceful warrior is only an apparent contradiction. He fights to bring peace within himself and around him.

We can define the quest for the peaceful warrior as the art of mastery over oneself by learning to adapt, learning to follow the course of things. It is a conscious process of transformation that leads to profound happiness; an inner state that cannot be reversed.

The deepest battle is to stop the calculations and open the heart. The expectation for immediate results, as inculcated by our education and our system of life, closes us from the inside and prevents us from proper conduct in the battle. I have found that when human beings cannot defend what is noble and just, they always accumulate tension that makes them aggressive and violent. It is then that selfishness takes precedence over altruism. These transference tactics are put in place when the human being can no longer act with the greatness of his soul. The path of the peaceful warrior aims to endow dignity to every human being. It is as old as our species.

An Immense Potential at Our Disposal

The way of the peaceful warrior, present in the ancient wisdom of the East and the West, teaches that each one of us, at the heart of our being, has an immense potential. This enables us to grow and to become better. Only the awakening and the actualization of this potential enables the development of the "knowledge-being". Three stages seem important for this actualization, which I can synthesize into three directives: to overcome oneself; to liberate oneself and others; to build and to be built.

To Overcome Oneself

In this stage, which is related to the art of the inner battle, we must become able to mobilize our own will. This means to implement courage and authenticity to apply the laws of life, teaching us to correct ourselves by extracting our latent potential. It is through the practice of discipline - which should not be rigid - that we will overcome inertia and gradually diminish our comfort zones. If we are motivated to express the true nature of our being, we will practice this new art of living, leading us to become the victorious warriors who defeat their own selves.

To Liberate Oneself and To Liberate Others

At this stage, we must learn to discern between what is useful and what is superfluous, by understanding our real needs. It is said that life is a journey in which one has to move without much weight. We must learn to unleash our energy which, in the Hindu and Buddhist tradition, is called *Virya*.

According to this theory, which in my experience has proven to be true, when someone is engaged with a cause, he discovers means he did not even suspect existed. Paradoxically, the practice of commitment lets loose new energies, such as the gift of the self, the gift of presence. One then possesses the real weapons, for which detachment is the key. With it, the opening of the heart becomes possible. And the best weapon becomes the ability to think with the heart, as explained in Egyptian thought, and as relayed to me by my master.

Expressing the good in oneself, and sharing that goodness with others, produces an extraordinarily purifying effect. We become detached from external thoughts, prejudices, critical judgments and useless comparisons. As in Plato's cave, we gradually release ourselves from our chains to face the light of day - reality as it is. At that moment the warrior is born, the liberator of mankind. For it is not possible to help others, if we have not already had the same experience ourselves.

To Build and To Be Built

The pursuit of the True and the Good helps us take the first steps. The concepts of the Just and the Beautiful can inspire us to build ourselves. Intelligence is the potential that awakens, making us capable of discerning and directing all of our mental abilities. Discernment allows us to see beyond appearances and, with the help of love-will, penetrate the inner nature of things, where true knowledge resides.

At that moment, an awareness emerges within us: we are not alone, we are interdependent with other human beings and with nature. We will now learn that in order to find the right expressions, in order to be and to act at the same time, we must reject tension and any form of rigidity. It is the respect and understanding of certain inner laws of nature that will soften our souls and give us the right expression.

At this point the warrior-constructor of civilizations appears.

The Four Dark Allies

A very important teaching explains that, like the actors of ancient Greek theater, we all wear a mask, thanks to which we can recognize the characters of a play. The mask expresses our knowledge in a certain way and gives us a personal dimension. It is this personality which should be at the service of the soul, the channel through which we must express our life-skills.

Our mask is composed of four elements: our physical body, our energies, our emotional body (emotions and feelings) and our rational or analytical mind.

As we know, our personality is mostly driven by possessions or desire. But sometimes it is capable of real openness and able to accommodate our inner voices and our potential actualization. Then it transmits nobility and dignity. The personality is naturally attracted to immediate results, and even though it is fascinated by beautiful things and great thoughts, when faced with the trials of existence, it can become deaf to the voices of the being, and think it can resolve the fights with the aid of what my master called the "dark allies".

I have already mentioned the pursuit of comfort and inertia that lies deep within our physical body or the state of distraction which makes us waste a lot of energy. But the real dark allies hide elsewhere. They speak to us and advise us as if they were true sages, confusing our consciousness with the lure of immediate gain. Anger and vulnerability hide in the meanderings of our emotions.

Anger

Anger is a powerful force of rejection. It separates us from others, because we think we are the victim of injustice. In reality, we are indignant at ourselves because of our own mistakes or at adverse circumstances and people. Initially, of course, anger can help us by giving us strength and a certain feeling of power. But, like all emotions, it doesn't last long and is insufficient to completely solve the problem. The trial will not be completely overcome. And this will engender a new seed of anger.

Vulnerability

Vulnerability is paradoxically complementary to anger. It is connected to attachment and suspicion. It feeds on an excessive love for one's own image and a feeling of being constantly judged. It can permanently disrupt our affective dimension. Pride and intolerance hide in the folds of our mental universe.

Pride

Pride relates to our narcissistic ego, which must not be confused with our innermost I, or Self. It is expressed through arrogance and vanity and makes us think that we are someone because we have responsibilities, functions or a noble birth. The proud individual is constantly afraid of ridicule. He will always be in search of social acceptance and will constantly repeat "that he must be up to the task". His behavior will lead to rigidity and an inability to adapt. Wanting to be perfect, we forget that first we must go through a process of continuous improvement. And this means learning from our own failures.

Intolerance

Intolerance is related to rejection, just as pride relates to attachment. The intolerant person is stubborn, inflexible and hardheaded. He sees himself as perfect and does not accept his mistakes, even when they are pointed out to him. He would like to constantly hide his errors and weaknesses. The intolerant person is incapable of assimilating an idea or a person. But above all, the intolerant person cannot assimilate his own errors or his own frailties. He cannot be corrected. He cannot learn to learn and hides his weakness under armor.

The voices of the four dark allies are always present to advise us with erroneous strategies and the false victories they bring. These voices want us to believe that we are always right and that we are the best, so to speak. With them, there is no need to question or observe oneself, or to let go of stubbornness. The four dark allies cause terrible suffering deep within the self, permanently altering the soul. As Plato already explained, when the soul is altered, it loses touch with itself and distorts reality, preventing itself from being part of it.

The Four Remedies

Every remedy on this path opens the door to an inner state.

Calmness and Determination

Calmness and determination can help us curb anger. To do this, we must learn to breathe. Breathing not only gives oxygen to our cells but also restores rhythm to the mind and the psyche. Together with slow and quiet breathing, slow movements teach us patience as well. Different traditions have developed various techniques. Regardless of which one is used, the important thing is to breathe calmly. This calm patience will help us decide, as well as to channel the energy of the nascent anger. Braving the force of rejection, we connect with ourselves and with the universe, the source of all creativity.

Self-affirmation and Tolerance

Basing our self-assurance on ourselves and not on others frees us from vulnerability. People who are sure of themselves will never feel hurt by what others say about them or how they look at them. They will become tolerant. The tolerance in question is not passive; that is to say, it does not imply doing nothing and being left alone. Active tolerance is benevolent; it leads us to share with others, taking into account differences, if there are any.

Humility of the Heart and Self-confidence

Humility of the heart fights pride and detaches the personal ego from narcissism. Pride is not self-confidence, but is its opposite. When you are confident, you do not need to put yourself on a pedestal. Self-confidence is a deep determination that allows us to act while being aware of our frailties.

Temperance and Living Together

The practice of temperance and moderation distances us from intolerance and hubris, the belief that we are superior to others. It opens up the way to co-existing with others. But co-existing does not just mean placing people next to each other, each looking towards a different direction. In the way of the peaceful warrior, living together is to accept others and to share with them. It allows us to emerge from our selfishness and to practice altruism.

This practice has made human beings and societies better since the dawn of humanity.

These remedies, which allow us to transcend our circumstantial states of mind, were called "virtues" by the ancients. The word "virtue" comes from the Latin *vir*, which indicates the strong, powerful, active part of ourselves.

In Greek it is called *arete*, which was related to the god Ares, the warrior, but also, to his appearance as the ram who pushes back darkness, breaking through closed doors and obstacles.

Arete is also associated with the plow and tillage. It is the ability to dig and leave furrows in the soil in order to make it fertile, to allow seeds to grow, to allow the potential symbolized by the seed to become a reality, like the harvested wheat.

For the Greeks as well as for the Romans, virtue was an inner force which leads to excellence, which leads to the best of ourselves, through the inner battle. The virtues are our allied army; it is for us to make good use of them.

CHAPTER III

The Three Faces of the Peaceful Warrior

The Bhagavad Gita:
The Warrior Who Conquers Himself

The *Bhagavad Gita* ("The Song of the Blessed") is an essential chapter of the Hindu epic, the *Mahabharata*, "The Great Battle of the Bharata Family". It is equivalent to the Greek *Iliad*. The teachings of the *Bhagavad Gita* can be summarized as: first to forget the self, then to act, and finally to participate in the collective destiny which we cannot avoid, whichever society we belong to.

In the ancient poem of *Bhagavad Gita*, Hindu wisdom explains that the inner battle takes place in the battlefield of our weaknesses, the *Kurukshetra*[21] (literally "the field of Kuru"). The immense army of the *Kuravas* represents the dark allies of our personality. Opposing them are the *Pandavas*, the sons of Pandu, who symbolize our virtues. The most valiant of Pandu's sons is Arjuna, the great archer, guided by his master Krishna, his coachman. The two armies battle over Hastinapura, the city of elephants, the city of wisdom.

---

21 Also called "the field of the fulfillment of *Dharma*" or "the field of the fulfillment of the Universal Law". To overcome our weaknesses, we must act in harmony with the laws of nature.

Arjuna recognizes his relatives, his own family among the thousands of warriors facing him. In effect, they are part of his personality. Why kill them, if they are a part of him? Overwhelmed with doubt, he asks Krishna to lead him to the middle of the battlefield to have a better look at the facing armies in order to decide whether he should go into the battle. After many hesitations and false considerations, Arjuna understands that his difficulty to charge into combat comes from his erroneous position: "It is poorness of spirit [pusillanimity] that has smitten away from me my (true heroic) nature, my whole consciousness is bewildered in its view of right and wrong."[22]

Pusillanimity means cowardice, lack of courage. Let us not forget that courage is the central virtue of the combatant. But pusillanimity also means being narrow-minded, stingy, such that actions are calculated for personal gain, rather than for the community. Such a position ultimately leads to softness, comfort, inertia.

With these words, Arjuna defines the essence of the peaceful warrior's action plan. The origin of our limitations lies in the narrowness of our feelings and our mind. And the first step to accomplish is to summon the will, together with the courage, to fight our own weaknesses.

His master Krishna reminds him that deep within he is a warrior, a *kshatriya* for whom there is no greater good than a just battle. Is there a more just battle than freeing oneself from pettiness and ignorance?

"When such a battle comes to them of itself like the open gate of heaven, happy are the Kshatriyas then."[23]

---

22 The Bhagavad Gita. Translated by Sri Aurobindo. Chapter II, Verse 7
23 Ibid. Chapter II, Verse 32

Then Krishna explains to Arjuna the meaning of this battle: "Thou hast a right to action, but only to action, never to its fruits; let not the fruits of thy works be thy motive, neither let there be in thee any attachment to inactivity. Fixed in Yoga do thy actions, having abandoned attachment, having become equal in failure and success; for it is equality that is meant by Yoga."[24]

You might get a good or bad result. The important thing is to act and learn from it to make progress.

"In him whose mind dwells on the objects of sense with absorbing interest, attachment to them is formed, from attachment arises desire; from desire anger comes forth. Anger leads to bewilderment, from bewilderment comes loss of memory; and by that the intelligence is destroyed: from destruction of intelligence he perishes."[25]

To prevent our inner being from dying, we must awaken and encourage its intelligence and discernment, which is capable of distinguishing the whole from the part. The aim of the battle is to give birth to the human being capable of discerning and acting intelligently in his or her work.

"Not by abstention from works does a man enjoy actionlessness, nor by mere renunciation (of works) does he attain to his perfection (to *siddhi*, the accomplishment of the aims of his self-discipline by Yoga). For none stands even for a moment not doing work, everyone is made to do action helplessly by the modes born of *Prakriti*. [Matter, which acts in the constant dialectic of deficiency, balance, excess]."[26]

---

24 Ibid. Chapter II, Verses 47-48
25 Ibid. Chapter II, Verses 62-63
26 Ibid. Chapter III, Verses 4-5

The Voice of the Silence: The Warrior Liberator of Mankind

At the end of the nineteenth century, after returning to the West, H.P. Blavatsky (H.P.B.), who had spent three years in monasteries between Nepal and present-day Tibet, transcribed and translated 39 small treaties out of the 90 chapters of the legendary *Book of Golden Precepts*, attributed to the Buddhist monk Aryasanga, a preacher and reformer of Buddhism who lived in the first centuries of the Christian era.

These precepts were intended for the everyday use of *lanoos*, disciples.

The *Book of Golden Precepts* claims the same origin as the great mystical work *Paramârtha* (or *Prajnaparamita*), which, according to legend, was given to the great Adept Nâgârjuna, by the *Nagas* or "Serpents", a name given to the initiates in ancient times.

The original Precepts are engraved on thin rectangular plates, and their copies are usually engraved on discs. These discs or plates are generally preserved on the altars of the temples attached to the centers where the so-called "contemplative" or *Mahâyâna* (*Yogâchâra*) schools are established.

According to H.P.B., the Voice of Silence, or *Nada*, can be translated as the "Mute Sound", which lies at the heart of sound. Its sound allows contact with the divine. It is only when true silence is reached that it becomes possible to hear this Voice, rising from our unfathomable depths. At that moment, the disciple is able to leave the world of *Asat*, of appearances, of falsehoods, of illusions, in order to enter the world of *Sat*, the true, which in reality is the Being, that which is, and is eternal.

This work is not only mystical but is also martial,

because the text unequivocally evokes the importance of the inner battle.

"Strive with thy thoughts unclean before they overpower thee. Use them as they will thee, for if thou sparest them and they take root and grow, know well, these thoughts will overpower and kill thee. Beware, Disciple, suffer not, e'en though it be their shadow, to approach. For it will grow, increase in size and power, and then this thing of darkness will absorb thy being before thou hast well realized the black foul monster's presence."[27]

This teaching also gives us an essential key: the path of our own evolution appears only when we start walking. There is no need to wait, and as long as we do wait, everything will remain theoretical and cause us considerable frustration. The steps we take towards our deepest being actualize the real power of our potential.

"Thou canst not travel on the Path before thou hast become that Path itself. Let thy Soul lend its ear to every cry of pain like as the lotus bares its heart to drink the morning sun. Let not the fierce Sun dry one tear of pain before thyself hast wiped it from the sufferer's eye."[28]

Moreover, she exhorts us to fight with extreme clarity:

"O thou anxious one, no warrior volunteering fight in the fierce strife between the living and the dead, not one recruit can ever be refused the right to enter on the Path that leads toward the field of Battle."[29]

In keeping with the lineage of the peaceful warrior, we

---

27 *The Voice of the Silence,* Translated and annotated by H.P. Blavatsky, I, 54
28 Ibid, I, 59-60
29 Ibid, II, 173

must live and transmit the path that leads to the *Kurukshetra*, the battlefield of our weaknesses. *The Voice of the Silence* is a reminder of this for the peaceful warriors, those who fight perseveringly for the liberation of mankind at all times and in all cultures.

"The fearless warrior, his precious life-blood oozing from his wide and gaping wounds, will still attack the foe, drive him from out his stronghold, vanquish him, ere he himself expires. Act then, all ye who fail and suffer, act like him; and from the stronghold of your Soul, chase all your foes away — ambition, anger, hatred, e'en to the shadow of desire — when even you have failed. . . Remember, thou that fightest for man's liberation, each failure is success, and each sincere attempt wins its reward in time. The holy germs that sprout and grow unseen in the disciple's soul, their stalks wax strong at each new trial, they bend like reeds but never break, nor can they e'er be lost. But when the hour has struck they blossom forth."[30]

"Wind, Sand and Stars" - "Citadel" – "Flight to Arras" The Warrior Builder of Civilizations

"Your task is not to foresee the future, but to make it possible." –Antoine de Saint-Exupery

As Laurent Ottavi[31] perfectly stated, Antoine de Saint-Exupery, on the eve of his death on the battlefield, wept over the decadence of a humanity deprived of all spirituality and devoured by a corrupting economic system.

"Man no longer has any meaning," deplores Saint-Exupery, because man no longer gives meaning, neither to himself nor to the world in which he does not live, but wanders, like a vagabond, in search of an illusionary material happiness: "He

30 Ibid, III, 273-274

31 *Letter to General X,* Laurent Ottavi, in libertépolitique.com

dies of thirst."

He speaks about the disappearance of art, in every one of its forms of expression, for the sake of calculation, technocracy, mathematics, and robotization. But he already foresees the colossal, existential post-war challenge that humanity will face: "Where is the United States going? And where are we going in this period of universal bureaucracy? The robot-man."

"You rolled yourself into a ball in your bourgeois security, your routines, the stifling rites of your provincial life, you raised this humble rampart against the winds and the tides and the stars. You do not want to worry about the big problems, you've had enough difficulty forgetting your condition as a man. You are not the inhabitant of a wandering planet, you do not ask yourself unanswered questions: you are a petty bourgeois from Toulouse. No one grabbed you by the shoulders when there was still time. Now the clay of which you are formed has dried and hardened, and no one amongst you can henceforth awaken the sleeping musician or the poet or astronomer who may have been at first dwelling in you. [...] But in the absence of new opportunities, for want of favorable ground, for want of a strict religion, they went back to sleep without believing in their own greatness."[32]

The misgivings of Saint-Exupery were confirmed by the system set up after the war, and which is now in decadence, victim of its own excessive materialism and technological sophistication, having left the human element behind. Indeed we live in a period of transition between two civilizations: one that has put man to sleep and another in which he may experience rebirth. Saint-Exupery says in his *Letter to the General*[33]: "The life of the spirit begins where we conceive a

---

32 *Wind, Sun and Stars,* Antoine de Saint-Exupery, Harcourt, 2002

33 *Letter of Saint-Exupery to General X,* written in Tunis in July 1943, and appears in the anthology *A Sense of Life*, Funk & Wagnalls, 1965

being beyond the materials constituting it."

And in *Flight to Arras*, he lays out the essential foundations necessary for rebuilding a civilization worthy of the human being.

"Civilization is an invisible good, since it is not concerned with things, but with the invisible bonds which tie them together, thus and not otherwise."[34]

"We must restore the Human Being. It is the essence of my culture. It is the key to my community. This is the principle of my victory."[35]

"You must give before receiving and build before you can live."[36]

In Citadel, Saint-Exupery insists that a civilization must first be built in the heart of man. For him, as for all peaceful warriors, civilization is not a set of systems or rules, but a state of consciousness, an inner state that allows us to grasp and to live a superior ideal that transcends individual selfishness. "If you want to build a boat, do not gather your men and women and give them orders, explain every detail, tell them where to find everything... If you want to build a boat, instill in the hearts of men and women the desire for the sea."[37]

He explains the logic of building a house or a civilization. It is not based simply on the logic of putting materials together but on a vision that lies in the architect's heart.

"Those who destroy their house with the pretension of knowing it, only have a pile of stones, bricks and tiles and

---

34 *Flight to Arras,* Antoine de Saint-Exupery, Harcourt Brace, 1969
35 Ibid.
36 Ibid.
37 *The Wisdom of the Sands,* Antoine de Saint-Exupery, 1950

are not familiar with the shadow, the silence, or the intimacy they are useful for, nor do they know what service to expect from this pile of bricks, stones and tiles, because they lack the invention that dominates the soul and the heart of the architect. For the stone lacks the soul and the heart of man. [...] I build my civilization, loving its only flavor, just as others write their poem and inflect the sentence and change the word, without being forced to justify the inflection or change, loving its only flavor, which they know by the heart."[38]

Saint-Exupery insists that "man discovers himself when he measures himself up with an obstacle." For trials mobilize our potential. The Warrior's way of building civilization is eternal. Yves Michaud defines civilization as the process of emerging from barbarism. This is the most important issue of today; we must re-establish links; links with ourselves, with humanity, with nature and with the universe. The warrior builder of civilization does not only think of himself and the people in his immediate surroundings. He feels the pain of all men and women of his country, and of humanity. When times are hard and the foundations that support society seem to be collapsing, the tendency is to retreat to safety and to conservatism, wishing to go back to the past rather than to build the future. Again, fear prevents us from seeing the future and from trusting the souls, not just of human beings, but of states. Yet, we have resources. Uniting an ideal of civilization with the soul of a country is an extraordinary tool for building the future.

It is, first of all, a symbolic battle, that of imagination: to see, act and believe differently.

For at the outset, civilizations are not built by conquering territories; we must first conquer the hearts and imagination of men. Their imagination will enable them to develop

38 Ibid.

alternative projects, built on the margins of the system but still in relation to it. These will help individuals become self-sufficient and transform the material world, but the human environment as well.

When the Western Roman Empire collapsed and cities were depopulated, the Cistercian monks created the concept of an abbey in the countryside. They taught the peasants who gathered around them how to select grains and improve agriculture. The abbeys thus created a new model of life that transformed the Dark Ages into civilization.

CHAPTER IV

The Peaceful Hero

The Hero Today

In our times, most great models of life have already collapsed. We used to believe that science will solve humanity's problems, such as disease, hunger, poverty and inequality. In the 60s and 70s, scientists, Nobel laureates, astronauts, politicians, prominent personalities such as Charles de Gaulle and John Fitzgerald Kennedy, and famous singers and actors, were sources of inspiration and role models. Today, corruption and scandals of all kinds (drugs, prostitution of minors, etc.) arouse general mistrust.

Apart from a few exceptions, such as Nelson Mandela, inspiring individuals are no longer around. Few role models can be cited who encourage men and women to follow and surpass themselves by following their example. But the need for that is still here; heroes continue to fare well. Cinemas fill up when a film shows a character who successfully incarnates courage, honor, and chivalry. The need for inspiration, the need to go beyond oneself, remains, although beyond fiction no one believes in it anymore and in everyday life mistrust prevails. We live in an apathetic society, withdrawn into itself, conservative and fainthearted, not to mention the social depression that has set in.

But the creativity, the courage, and the desire to be a pioneer, which was scary ten years ago, is reappearing on the margins of our society through alternative projects aiming to successfully continue the transition of civilization.[39]

In a time so full of doubt and mistrust, in which it is so difficult to live in solidarity, the only honest and judicious proposal that can be made, without risking the manipulation and negation of the individual, or of self-deception and utopia, is the way of the peaceful warrior. It consists of awakening the hero that dwells within each one of us.

Otherwise, how can we restore individual self-confidence and social vigor? Within us are the means by which we can regain our confidence and live a life that is less bland, less dull and less mediocre; more lively, rich and colorful. Let us not forget that whatever people say, every person is born with the feeling that he has something to accomplish, and every person feels, at least subconsciously, the need to leave something behind, to be someone, and to earn respect.

The journey of the peaceful warrior consists precisely of finding within the means to realize this intuition that we all share. The heroic path requires us to take on the trials and challenges to make it happen.

The Greeks defined the hero as the individual who becomes conscious, not only of having a certain life span, but of a destiny to accomplish.

---

39 See the films *A Quest for Meaning*, by Nathanaël Coste and Marc de la Ménardière, produced by Kamea Meah and *Tomorrow (Original Title: Demain)* by Cyril Dion and Mélanie Laurent, produced by Mars Films.

There Is a Potential Hero Within Each of Us...

Each of us is potentially a hero, that is, someone who seizes a destiny, not a destiny that others impress upon us, but our own destiny, a destiny we feel we can accomplish in life. The number one quality of a hero lies in this statement: "I serve something, I have a role to play, a mission to fulfill. I have a destiny."

In this period of anonymity, everyone wants to be like the others; everyone seeks reassurance, and takes as little risk as possible. This is the most effective way of convincing ourselves that we are insignificant, in other words, of killing the hero within. "I am not useful for anything..." To feel this - not to hear oneself say it, but to believe it - is the worst thing that can happen. The notion of heroism is directly linked to the dignity of the peaceful warrior. To be someone; that is, to become oneself, not to the detriment of others, is every individual's most legitimate right to claim without shame.

The Everyday Hero

The heroism that we are all entitled to entails owning one's responsibilities in life, ceasing to flee, asserting oneself and moving forward. Heroism is not only about finding a new truth, but it is also to have the courage to implement that vision every day. The hero in question is not the hero of the movies or comic books, but a hero formed in everyday life - an everyday hero.

"When we believe our journeys are not important and when we do not face our dragons or seek our treasures, we feel empty inside, and that leaves a void that affects us all."

This mechanism, described by Carol S. Pearson[40], foments in the young and the not-so-young the pseudo-indifference

40 A myth expert, who wrote the book *The Hero Within: Six Archetypes we live by*, HarperElixir publishing, 368 pgs.

responsible for the spirit of derision which pervades the world today, as is evident in comic books and TV shows. The more this derision manifests, the more amorphous societies become, and the less individuals are motivated, and able, to take charge of themselves.

In this modern, uniform world, psychologists have a definition for the rare case of a person who is suffering from "illusions of grandeur," but not for the most widespread illness: "illusions of uselessness."

Although it is true that none among us is more important than another, we all have a valuable contribution to make, a quality, a goodness that we are unable to give if we do not start our journey...

We can live great lives only if we are willing to grow up and abandon the illusion of impotence by becoming responsible for our lives.

Feeling Legitimate and Rooted

Because of its linear view of time and its cult of novelty, modernity has brought about a perpetual change in ways of life, relentlessly destroying the points of reference formed by these ways of life. This resulted in the perception, both among individuals and in the collective subconscious, that actions have no substance or roots. Thus, the exaltation of one moment is often succeeded by a strong depression, as one realizes that the reference points of contemporary fashion are hollow and do not bring sufficient depth to generate a consistency of events.

Carol S. Pearson explains that in order to transcend this state, we must feel ourselves legitimately rooted both in history and in eternity. It is the only way to avoid falling into the blindness of action for action's sake or into escapism. The hero's quest is both rooted in the eternal principles of existence, which are reflected in myths and tales, and in a struggle that is taking place here and now. Structures, myths and stories are eternal. But the battle takes place in the present.

This implies, therefore, the need for understanding and accepting the world as it is, and at the same time the need for a solid awareness of the eternal roots of each person's narrative. This alone allows us to live authentically.

Rediscovering the Other Who Is In Us

One of the major problems of contemporary societies is the individual loss of confidence, whatever their age and condition. Are these individuals really worse than their ancestors? We don't think so. Today, most psychologists try to help people adapt to their feeling of impotence, which in the long run will only make them apathetic and passive. They are not encouraged to undertake the voyage to discover what they could be, to become that peaceful warrior we all feel we potentially are, the true protagonist within us. This implies a revolution to reveal the existence of other needs, deeper and more permanent, situated at the level of being, and not only of having and appearing.

The role of genuine psychologists and educators is to teach people about the existence of those other needs. By rediscovering them, they would gain access to a dimension of consciousness in which they would find respect for themselves and an awareness of their own legitimacy. This is not something that society or other people can give us. It leads to a true affirmation of ourselves, thanks to which our unique qualities can benefit the whole, without us becoming prisoners to validation from others.

The more we are ourselves, the more we can respect others and be useful to them. Constant imitation condemns us to mass culture and uniformity. The quest of the peaceful warrior leads us to free ourselves from inauthentic forms of life and to become real human beings who can let go of the artificial and superficial, and bring out our qualities so we can live our destiny.

Heroes Grow In the "Deserts of Meaning"

This is how Boris Cyrulnik[41], resilience[42] theorist, explains the birth of the hero. After studying emotional and social deficiencies in children, he realized that those who had the highly valuable element of resilience had all at one time identified themselves as a hero. In their soul, a shelter, a psychic enclave, allowed them to withstand, in order to repair themselves. After losing his parents at Auschwitz and escaping from the Gestapo at the age of six, Remi, from Malot's *Nobody's Boy* (*Sans Famille*), found refuge with heroes. So did Oliver Twist[43], the English orphan exploited by cruel adults, and *The Child*[44] of Jules Vallès, who defended the world against the wicked. These heroes brought magic to dilapidated childhoods. Boris Cyrulnik has taken up a formula drawn by Jules Michelet in his essay *La Sorcière* "heroes grow in the cultural chaos and the desert of meaning."

All heroes are models of resilience. Unfortunately, on the same planet, in the 21st century, there are other kinds of prosperous 'heroes', claiming to stand for a cause by massacring those who do not believe in it: terrorists. The lack of emotional and cultural support in childhood makes children vulnerable later to the rhetoric of the so-called savior.

---

41 French Psychologist and psychoanalyst who was born in 1937, author of numerous books, such as *Resilience: How Your Inner Strength Can Set You Free from the Past*, ed. Tarcher, 320 pages.

42 In physics, a body's ability to withstand shocks and regain its initial structure. In psychology, an individual's ability to overcome the painful moments of existence and to rebuild by growing out of it.

43 English novel by Charles Dickens (Oliver Twist or The Parish Boy's Progress), serialized between 1837 and 1839 in the journal Bentley's Miscellany.

44 A French Autobiographical novel by Jules Valles (1832 – 1885), 1st volume of a trilogy.

How can one resist a person who tells you: "Believe in me, I will save you," or better: "You will help us save the world." Such a hero is also the bearer of extreme ideologies, religious fundamentalism and other millenarian sects. For some of these children, who feel excluded from society, it is better to die as such a 'hero', inspiring terror, rather than to live in contempt. Through their propaganda videos, with well-defined codes that may put Hollywood to envy, Daesh's screenwriters have managed to create an emotional intensity that produces group contagion.

Boris Cyrulnik wisely draws an opposition between these visible, spectacular, eroticized heroes, in love with death - because they don't have any other way of becoming - and the resisting hero who stands in the shadows, like the powerful example of Germaine Tillion,[45] a woman and a resistance fighter who, unlike those 'heroic martyrs' and slaughterers, wanted to live. The true hero is willing to sacrifice himself to save others, without seeking death. Boris Cyrulnik, like others, believes that in our disenchanted societies, we should restore measured risk and initiation rites, practice volunteering in foreign NGOs, volunteer to restore natural parks, and finally, recover a strong self-esteem in order to protect ourselves from the temptation of totalitarianism.

45 French writer and ethnologist (1907-2008), having performed many heroic acts during the Second World War he was buried in the Pantheon in 2015 with National honors.

CHAPTER V

The Shadows and Light of the Warrior

Today, with the ideologies of terror, dark heroes who deny life have acquired a power of seduction over certain orphaned youth and, in some cases, criminals. Why are dark heroes so seductive in contemporary society? Journalist Bill Moyers[46] asked mythologist Joseph Campbell what happens when a society no longer elaborates a powerful and structuring mythology, and he replied, "You only have to read the newspaper to see the reprehensible and violent actions carried out by young people who do not know how to behave in a civilized society. In reality, society has not provided them with the rituals to enable them to become members of the community in their own right."

"All children need a second birth. They must learn to behave rationally in today's world, leaving their childhood behind...From where do kids get their myths now? ... They create them themselves. Hence all the graffiti that we see on city walls. These kids form their own tribes, with their own

46 Conversations realized in 1987 between journalist Bill Moyers and Joseph Campbell for the book The Power of Myth, published by Anchor in 1991.

initiatory rites, their own morality...Only, they are dangerous, for their laws are not ours. They were not socially initiated."[47]

A few decades later, Islamism, the Marxism of the twentieth century, is offering them diverted heroic myths. But what makes them work?

In all myths there is an incarnation of the destructive forces of human nature. But after countless battles and trials, these forces are defeated by a hero who represents the constructive forces of good. Heroes are supposed to become a model and a reference of exemplary behavior to imitate. They demonstrate, in all cultures, the way in which social initiation allows the integration and acceptance of individuals into the community. The need for trials, for a confrontation with oneself, in order to actualize what one is, is inherent in human nature. But our present societies no longer offer adequate rites of passage for youth, leaving the door open to the dark aspects of the archetypes.

Archetypes, or spiritual and psychic models, have always been present in our collective subconscious. Unfortunately, however, depending on the level of consciousness with which we grasp them, they can be a source of inspiration for either the best or the worst. Psychiatrist Carl G. Jung had discovered that archetypes expressed themselves on several levels. When our consciousness comes into contact with the boundaries of the subconscious, a guardian of the threshold appears in order to test how determined we are to cross through the threshold into the invisible realm. It looks fierce, a concentrated form of our repressions – dark emotions or thoughts we cannot accept as part of ourselves. It is the archetype of the shadow, the first step of the internal struggle.

47 The sacred camouflaged or the symbolic crisis of the present world, Fernand Schwarz, Éditions Cabédita, 2014, 120 pages, page 15

The Shadow

Archetypes don't have only a positive aspect. Like everything in this world, they also have a negative aspect, which is their shadow. The many negative aspects of the archetypes are perfectly symbolized in the image of the multi-headed dragon, which epitomizes the many faces of the dragons every hero must fight during his journey, and the challenges each of us faces. In the tales, these dragons block the hero's passage, guard some treasure, or kidnap a princess. They are both the obstacle and the key. To defeat the dragon is, in a certain way, to seize its strength, to master a power hitherto impossible to grasp. The force which it represents and which appears to be negative, once integrated, becomes beneficial and civilized.

The trials of existence always impress their terrifying side upon us. The acquisition of a new quality depends directly on our ability to face the call of the shadow, the dragon, the negative side of the archetype.

The shadow beckons us through the situations we refuse to face. This refusal entraps us in the chaotic and destructuring abyss of the archetype's shadow. To identify the stage we are in, we must remember that we don't love or desire what we have, but what we lack. It is by trying to understand the shadow of each archetype that we are expressing, that we can situate ourselves. It helps us to accept the things we suppress and the situations we live in - everything that prevents us from becoming a complete being. Progress does not consist of rejecting or repressing more and more aspects of ourselves, but rather in recognizing and accepting our less flattering sides, while remaining conscious of the qualities we carry within us because through them we can bring about reconciliation with ourselves.

The Journey Of The Peaceful Warrior: THE PREPARATION

1) The Preparation: To eliminate dependence and lack of differentiation. To defeat the ego.		
ARCHETYPE	SHADOW	TEACHINGS
The Innocent Child Confidence in life	Staying soft under all circumstances. Fear of abandonment. Negation / repression of problem.	To take responsibility over the reality of life, to leave naiveté behind, to develop patience and optimism.
The Malcontent Live the contradictions	The orphan, the victim who does not take responsibility. Fear of being exploited.	To accept suffering and understand its causes. To become responsible and find a place.
The Martial Warrior To choose the right battle	The bellicose warrior. Seeking personal power. Wanting to win at all costs.	To accept the trials. To follow the rules of the game, leave violence behind. To assume adversity.

The Journey Of The Peaceful Warrior: THE JOURNEY

2) The Journey: To become the captain of one's soul		
ARCHETYPE	SHADOW	TEACHINGS
Solidarity Being Opening the heart	The martyr: Ensures and maintains his power by playing the savior, but infantilizing and stifling those he helps.	To open the heart and become sensitive to the suffering of others. Openness and generosity.
The Adventurer Being a dolphin	Perfectionism, difficulty to commit, consumer in flight prone to all dependencies.	Autonomy in the management of conflicts and trials. Perseverance in the quest for meaning.
The Peaceful Warrior The power of commitment	Avidity, jealousy arising from the need to compare and be recognized. Possessive and seductive. Victim of one's projections.	To purify the heart. Devotion and fidelity to one's commitment, whatever the difficulties are. Purification and regeneration.

The Journey Of The Peaceful Warrior: THE RETURN

3) The Return: The mysteries of transformation.		
ARCHETYPE	SHADOW	TEACHINGS
The Mystes The destroyer of old forms.	Auto-destruction. The lack of self-esteem that leads to the destruction of others and to excesses of all kinds.	Detachment through the virtue of humility. To recognize one's shadows and one's dragons and transform the consciousness by accepting death.
The Link To be oneself	Inner simmering which prevents putting anything into practice in a sustainable way. Activist who hates emptiness, workaholic.	To discover one's own law of action, one's profound vocation. Expression of the inner man in one's choices and behaviors in the world.
The Wisdom Warrior	The tyrant who wants to control everything, trampling the dignity of the others.	To help others find the meaning of their deep self while cultivating their own. Awakening of internal power. To assume complete responsibility for one's life.

The Three Levels of Finding Archetypes

In her study, Carol S. Pearson observes that the ascent from the depths of our inner abyss is not automatic and that each archetype has at least three possible levels of reaction, depending on a person's degree of consciousness. The first is that of the ego: moved by the instinct of survival, one assumes the archetype at the level of one's egoistical self, for the shadow is still powerful. At the second level, the individual transcends their egocentrism, no longer acts only in their own interest, and opens himself up to the meaning of things and to the consequences of their actions, assuming responsibility for themselves and for others. Finally, at the third transpersonal level, the individual is detached and listens to others. They become the channel of the archetype.

The hero's journey is to be understood as a crossing of a sea. Despite the constants of life and even though we all take part in the same journey, of birth and death, our roads do not overlap in the immense ocean of life and psyche.

Each archetype is an inspiring model, an advisor, a bearer of trials. To integrate it with ourselves, we need a constant desire to elevate from shadows to light. In reality, as we have seen, it is always the same archetype. It is we who can live it differently by changing our inner position. This forces us to leave behind all forms of rigidity and to create inner movement, until we arrive at the right place to discover its wisdom and its liberating nature, which is in fact our center, the highest part of ourselves. In this sense, the journey comprises both of navigation through the waters of life and of an ascent to the heart of our own inner mountain.

From Shadows to Light, Archetypes of the Warrior

We will illustrate this by presenting the most widespread heroic archetype seen today in literature, cinema or the arts: The *Warrior.*

The shadow of the *Warrior* is the person who lives this archetype, but in order to obtain personal benefits, rather than the greater good, and without any moral or ethical considerations. This shadow can also be activated in our lives whenever we yield to the temptation to deny our values in order to achieve and get what we desire, in terms of having or possessing more. The Shadow of the *Warrior* reigns in today's economic world where the pursuit of profit at all costs, without concern for ecological, human or social consequences is causing havoc.

Another aspect of the Warrior's shadow, employed by terrorists, is the tendency of permanent conflict wherein one is constantly confronted with the threat, aggression, challenge, contempt and fear of an enemy which can come from anywhere. Today's world lives this shadow of the Warrior, which is the opposite of any chivalrous ideal.

The Warrior's Call

Calls are situations in which the archetype's shadow summons us. In the case of the *Warrior,* this call is a confrontation with what he feels to be a challenge. On the first level, the answer is to fight for oneself, or for others, but for personal ends, disregarding all rules. On the second level, the struggle for oneself, and for others, takes into account the rules of the game, with an altruistic perspective. On the third level, after inner stability has been established, one fights for what is really worthwhile. One is able to prioritize, to pass from just fighting, to fighting for the essential things, without seeking personal victory. Violence becomes less necessary. This stage leads us to win-win situations. We lay all our cards on the table. In accordance to the situations we are facing, at the second and third levels we can hear new calls that summon us to help and protect others and to become aware of our dependence on them.

New conflicts emerge at that point: linking one's own needs with those of others, distrusting oneself, taking care of oneself, not being destabilized by the environment, not to take the same care of ourselves. The gifts we receive from the Warrior are the discipline and courage that prepare us to live with discernment, generosity and compassion.

Our individual response to each of the archetypes of the journey varies. This explains why someone, depending on the circumstances, may appear inferior to himself or on the contrary, superior. This is due to the fact that he is not in alignment with the archetype corresponding to the situation or that he is living it at a different level. One can also fall while moving forward on the path. Either the defect is so powerful that he is caught by the shadow, or during the fall, the level of consciousness acquired by the individual creates a force that calls the individual upward and makes it possible to resume the journey.

In the hero's journey we find, above all, the treasure of one's true and profound being, in order to ultimately return home and share it to help transform the kingdom and one's own life, as Carol Pearson essentially says. "The mission in itself is lined with perils and obstacles but brings great rewards: the ability to be successful in the world, the knowledge of the mysteries of the human soul, the opportunity to find and express our unique gifts to the world and to live in a union of love with those around us."[48]

48 Awakening the Heroes Within, Carol S. Pearson, HarperSanFransisco, 1991

CHAPTER VI

The Heroic Journey of the Peaceful Warrior

"The hero's journey is nothing but the self-improvement project, it is a tool to meet and honor all that is true in relation to oneself."[49]

The Tragic Dimension of the Heroic Path: Undertaking Trials

On the level of imagination, we perceive our path as a voyage between two horizons, one bearing the image of birth and the other, of death. It is a path filled simultaneously with pitfalls, trials and satisfactions, and which leads us to experience all the aspects of existence, achievements as well as failures, thanks to which our identity matures, our consciousness grows and our existence acquires meaning. Even if this journey is realized in keeping with an immutable scenario that integrates the constants of the human condition, the path of the peaceful warrior enables each person to live an original, different, life, by implementing, in the face of circumstances, the qualities that are one's own.

The myths of different civilizations present the essential

49 Awakening the Heroes Within, Carol S. Pearson, HarperSanFransisco, 1991.

scenarios of existence, the challenges they imply, and their meaning, in order to give mankind, not only models, but also reference points. They are like inner guides that advise and inspire us through the trials. Although bequeathed to us by very different cultures, they all express the constants of universal human nature.

It is for this reason that, despite their seemingly primitive appearance, they can help us let go of inauthentic ways of life and transform into our real selves.

The peaceful warrior is the man, or woman, who is able to go through the cycle of trials by developing the ability to free the self from the artificial and superficial. In doing so, his intrinsic qualities emerge making him capable of living his destiny.

Accepting destiny gives the heroic path its tragic dimension, as is expressed very well by the Greek tragedies. As Jorge Angel Livraga pointed out, the Greeks, especially Aeschylus[50], had the best theoretical and pedagogical approach to the subject at hand.

Greek theater, in its profound, metaphysical sense - that of the Mystery Theater, or the true theater of life - invites us to tear ourselves away from the illusion of appearance, in order to become the profound being that we truly are. "The Mystery Theater is fundamentally educational. There is always, in whichever of its genres, the intention of teaching something and, especially in the case of tragedy, of overwhelming, surprising and capturing the attention of the spectator in such a way that he ceases to be one. Gradually, he finds himself becoming part of the work itself, as if he were another of

50 One of the most ancient Greek tragedians (circa 526 BC - 456 BC) He participated in the establishment of the Greek tragedy. Author of about 110 pieces of which only 7 were transmitted to us, among which are the Orestia.

the actors, or at least a participant deeply affected by the events… Its ideal was that the spectator would go through a transformation."[51]

It is up to each one of us to gradually understand that the tragic dimension is the space-time in which every peaceful warrior lives.

Today, the word tragedy is associated with the idea of death, misfortune, or catastrophe. With this understanding of the concept we have retained only the appearance of the original, for in reality there are always two ways to respond to tests: the first is to refuse to face them, which then triggers hubris and excess, which in turn brings on blindness and the desire to escape one's destiny. Then tragedy ensues, in accordance with the way it is perceived today.

The second way we can respond to tests is the heroic way. In this way, instead of being a victim, the hero takes on the trial and, surpassing himself, overcomes it. The laws of fate, which appeared to be against him, dragging him into the depths of the underworld, are reversed at the most difficult moment to become a force of elevation and ascension, acting in his service. It is arduous but necessary to learn that these laws, which manifest in the scenes of heroic myths, are the stages of the journey and the inner guides at the same time.

Triumph over Death

The essence of tragedy is the triumph over death. The first teaching of the Mysteries of Dionysus, the Greek god who gave birth to theater, was to learn to free oneself from fear, the greatest of which is the fear of death. The letting go that this entails is the heroic womb. Behind the Greek tragedies lies a profound teaching of inner awakening.

---

51 The Mystery Theatre in Greece – Tragedy, Jorge Angel Livraga, New Acropolis UK, 1987, pg. 15.

"Aeschylus is so didactic that, for example, when referring to a crime, he develops it as a mere excuse to show the deep causes which led to such a fatal action and what will come of it, following the flow of action and reaction which is in the nature of the cosmos. He is attempting to reveal the Essences, which is typical of the Mysteries, since in those so-called 'Mysteries' the aim of the Initiates was, above all, for the neophytes to go into themselves, not as islands, but as joined up and interdependent parts, in the visible and in the invisible worlds, within the Whole of the cosmos."[52]

These words give a measure of the heroic feat: when events make us lose control under the effect of fear or anger – both are forms of excess – to be able to regain control, to refocus and to gain access to a different state of consciousness.

"The initiation in the Mysteries could accelerate the process by achieving a transmutation of certain factors, such as time. Unleashed hidden forces, passions which rise up like prehistoric monsters, control of the mind and therefore of the situation, perception of one's own immortal and invulnerable spirit, living contact with all the manifested and non-manifested forms of nature and with the soul of nature itself, the Great Mother, gave the neophyte the opportunity of being initiated and reborn without having passed the portals of death, as often as his own capacity allowed."[53]

This new perspective on the theme should encourage those wishing to take their first steps on the path of transformation, to see the myths, Greek or others, in a new light, taking into account the archetypes they contain.

Thus, the understanding of the tragic dimension allows us to read the myths, and to avoid a partial reading, be it social,

52 Ibid, pg. 44
53 Ibid, pg. 45

historical or economic. It is the key that gives them their true depth. The inner guides are archetypes that have accompanied human beings since the beginning of time. Their reflections are found in art, literature, religion, etc., and the fact that they are found in all cultures proves that they are indeed archetypes. They are primordial forces and modes of behavior that outline life and show us how to live. These guides are sometimes seen as gods or goddesses present in the collective subconscious. They nourish and inspire our psyche. That is why we can find them within ourselves, in our own dreams and reveries, as well as in our actions. But we can meet them also outside, in myths, legends, art, literature, religion, etc. They give us images of our inner heroes, beyond our limitations.

From the perspective of inner growth, the archetypes act as guides in our quest. Each of the archetypes that manifests in our lives brings with it both a mission and a teaching, essentially a gift that is sanctioned by a trial, just like the treasure of fairytales. The archetypes we encounter in our lives represent the roles we will have to incarnate during our journey. In the same way an actor is called to play various characters, diverse as the roles we play in the course of our lives, in the spheres of family, business, and so on. Archetypes enable us to assume and better embody the multiple facets of our lives as well as their contradictions.

Insofar as we play these roles, as imposed upon us by the journey, we develop various social skills that awaken new qualities of our being. "The soul lies beyond its masks and its different sets of clothes. The Initiatic theater is not made only for the spectators, but fundamentally for the artists, who are initiated by this means (...) For artists, making their characters live and die is what makes them aware of and allows them to experience their permanence beyond changes and circumstances."[54]

---

54 Ibid, pg. 157

The Three Stages of the Journey

The peaceful warrior's approach is always that of a traveler. This journey, or crossing, is comprised of three stages: the preparation, the crossing and the return.

Preparation

During the preparatory phase, the peaceful warrior discovers his or her tools and learns to use them. This preparation usually takes place in the fringes of society, in rupture with the natural environment, in relation to a sometimes seemingly negative situation, such as the death of parents, abduction, abandonment, etc. Or it begins when an ordeal of suffering ends a happy period. Even in the case of a departure marked by pain, this preparatory phase appears as a golden age, a kind of childhood, a period of learning. In a television series, the eruption of evil which destroys happiness will mark the beginning of the story, a brutal break that triggers the crossing, the central phase of the journey. Having lost security, being left to oneself, without a visible guide, one is forced to appeal to one's own memory, to one's inner resources. At that point the real trials appear, during which no one can give consolation. During the preparatory phase, one acquires skills to project and identify oneself.

The Crossing

The crossing becomes harder and enables the awakening of the true identity and one's own way of action. During the crossing, the skills acquired appear only as means. The clarity of the goal and the ability to remain confident despite adversity become imperative. It is the moment when, as victims of our dark side, we have to face the dragons. The shadow is unleashed because we are vulnerable and unprotected. In the first part of our journey, this shadow tests us and subjects us to mirages. One discovers then that the true enemy lies within oneself. This ends only when the dragon is finally defeated and the dark side becomes light. In stories, this victory is shown as the acquisition of treasure, or the acquisition of particular gifts: it is the discovery of the Grail.

The Return

The return corresponds to the reintegration into society and the world order. The hero returns and shares with society what he has acquired, by participating in its governance. At that point in the tales, the hero ascends to the throne, marries and brings about prosperity. Although the journey began with a rupture, it ends with reintegration and participation in developing social harmony. Indeed, the heroic journey does not end at victory. It has value only if it becomes valuable for society and if the triumph is shared with the group to which the hero belongs. A situation that began in destabilization eventually leads to a higher equilibrium.

This journey is not a loop on a horizontal plane. Instead, it is a spiral path. It is not only an individual accomplishment of the hero himself, but of the entire community, and as such it represents a benefit to the whole. The hero is usually thought of as an individual on the fringes of society, an outsider, whereas what's at stake is the reintegration of an accomplished individual into society. The heroic quest is the best way an individual can go through a process of socialization without falling into anonymity and homogenization.

All adolescents dream of heroism, but when integrated into adult life they see themselves compelled to look just like everyone else, and to anesthetize or kill the hero within. They have no option but to live indirectly and to become spectators of B movies. But this ultimately only increases frustration. The alternative is to reconnect with their intimate, ever-present conviction, however much it may have been stifled, in order to undertake, against all odds, the quest of the inner hero, in search of oneself and ultimately, of a true world.

CHAPTER VII

The Nine Trials and the Nine Victories

In different traditions, the hero's journey was comprised of a different number of stages. But all included the idea of the three fundamental stages we have seen above: the preparation, the crossing and the return. Practical experience has shown me that a nine-step journey enables young people to embark onto the adventure and achieve positive results.

The preparation with its three trials makes us confront the personal ego and allows us to experience the first aspect of the peaceful warrior - the warrior who conquers himself. To prepare and to defeat the personal ego, even if only temporarily, is the starting point of any inner achievement.

The crossing draws us away from the possessive hold of the personal ego and leads us towards setting our souls free, fulfilling, at least partially, the second aspect of the peaceful warrior: the liberated and liberating warrior. The soul of which I speak of is the one mentioned by the ancient Greeks; it is an intermediary between our material dimension and our spiritual or profound being.

As the equivalent Latin word indicates (*anima*: the vital breath), it animates our actions. When we act with our soul, we project, we become involved, and we unlock something. The soul helps to open the heart. The Greeks called it the psyche, which can ascend and descend between the earthly world and the heavenly world. If we cannot elevate it, we cannot reach our depths or establish an inner dialogue. The return, with all its trials, gives us the opportunity to build a suitable inner vessel to channel our spirit through action in this world and to give birth to the third aspect of the peaceful warrior: the warrior-builder.

The first three archetypes we have to face in order to defeat our ego are: the Innocent Child, the Malcontent and the Martial Warrior.

The three archetypes of the crossing which liberate the soul are: the Solidarity Being, the Adventurer and the Peaceful Warrior.

And finally, the archetypes of the return are the expression of our spirit: The Mystes, the Link, and the Warrior of Wisdom.

This path aims to help us better understand our behavior and our attitudes towards life and its trials. It illuminates the role archetypes play in connecting the still unknown world of our inner self, with the known world of our behaviors and attitudes. These archetypes are images and inner symbols that speak to our imagination and with which our consciousness can dialogue to make sense of them.

PREPARATION:
TO LEAVE BEHIND DEPENDENCE AND LACK OF DISCERNMENT. DEFEAT THE EGO.

The Innocent Child

The archetype of the *Innocent Child* teaches us optimism,

trust and patience. It is the part of us that trusts life, trusts the self, and others. When adopted badly, this archetype can lead to a form of naive pacifism, a subconscious refusal to see the complexity of things. When the individual makes contact with the archetype of the *Innocent Child* from the shadow of the ego, he will be scared, as his only objective will be to remain safe in a world of pleasures and satisfactions.

On the other hand, this child, innocent and scared, will customize his character so that others will like him and be proud of him. He will be afraid of his first trials and will do anything to be accepted - including the denial of his own depth - which can then lead downwards, into the trap of manipulation.

By refusing to investigate the deeper nature of things, he can only remain on the surface, unable to face reality. He does not face the struggles of life and runs the risk of taking refuge in an artificial paradise, of drugs or alcohol, in order to live the dimension that he lacks by refusing the trials of reality. In this manner, he will often sacrifice the truth to safeguard his own interests, his comforts and his protected world.

To get moving, he will have to give up the view of the world as a playground for pleasure and satisfaction. In order to fulfill his ambition to become better, he will have to leave behind this period of life, which is proper for young children. He will have to learn to trust without being naive, develop cautious optimism, be loyal to his commitments, be patient in the face of trials and overcome the fear of leaving behind a sense of security in order to face reality.

In synthesis, the shadow of the *Innocent Child* is to remain *soft* at all costs. His fear is to be abandoned. He must learn discernment, experience the world in order to emerge from naivety and develop patience, trust and optimism.

The Malcontent: Living the Contradictions

Leaving innocence behind allows us to discover the world as it is. This is the time of learning, discovery and the need to connect with others. The shadow of the orphan can appear at this stage. The orphan poses as a victim, and does not assume responsibility. After leaving the cocoon and experiencing the fall, we feel abandoned, disillusioned, and betrayed by life, especially by those whom we believe should have helped us. We become the *Malcontent*, whose shadow is the orphan.

The archetype of the *Malcontent* teaches us to take responsibility for securing our own needs, and to stop asking others to be responsible for us. We realize the existence of others, besides us, though at first the others may seem threatening.

The *Malcontent* is rattled by a consciousness trapped in duality. He, and the others, and everything else, is marked by antagonism and separation in this world of permanent insecurity. Everything that is not as per his own projections or expectations seems unfair to him. The temptation during this phase is to mislead others in order to be right. The fear of impotence is pronounced, as well as the inner conflict which results from a lack of assertiveness that blocks everything.

This uncomfortable situation helps him develop attention, to keep alert. If he learns to trust others, he can regain his power. The *Malcontent* is a disappointed, wounded, deeply pained idealist, who seeks to conceal his pain by avoidance behaviors.

Under the pretense of weakness and a state of victimhood, the person controlled by this archetype always seeks to receive special treatment. His characteristic chronic anger triggers an attack on the very people who seek to help him. Cynical, masochistic or sadistic, he uses his role as a victim to manipulate.

As he gains confidence, he can consciously take responsibility for his wounds, gradually recover and heal, and emerge from his victimhood. His omnipresent fear of being exploited will disappear and an awareness of the interdependence of all beings will emerge.

In synthesis, the shadow of the *Malcontent* is the orphan, the victim who doesn't assume responsibility. The person who seeks security at all cost, always scared of being exploited. The *Malcontent* must learn to integrate suffering, understand its causes, and find his place by associating with others through links of interdependence and realism.

The Martial Warrior: Choosing the Right Battle

The time has come to accept the fight. The archetype of the Martial Warrior is not yet the archetype of the Peaceful Warrior, but with it the person accepts the battle and faces the trials of life.

With this archetype the preparation stage comes to an end; at this stage, one learns to set life goals and develop strategies that generally require discipline and courage, and acceptance of the rules of the game.

Discipline and courage prepare us to live with generosity and compassion. But in the beginning of this stage, when the personal ego fights against its shadows, the struggle is solely for one's own benefit, for personal ends, and with disregard for all rules. Then little by little the outlook widens, and the struggle for oneself, and for others, begins with the acceptance of the rules of the game.

When this stage is integrated and internal stability established, we then fight for what is really worthwhile. We are able to prioritize and to fight for the essential. Violence is no longer necessary. The candidate accepts the necessity of combat in the face of adversity.

The shadow of the Martial Warrior is the bellicose warrior, who seeks power for personal gain, wishing to conquer for one's own benefit at the expense of the greater good, and uses power for personal ends, with absolute contempt for all ethics. One recognizes this in the obsessive need to conquer and win at all costs. Anyone else is an opponent to be defeated, and is a threat. Hence the tendency for permanent conflict, aggressiveness, challenge, and contempt.

In synthesis, the shadow of the *Martial Warrior* is to want triumph at all cost. In fact, he fears his own weakness and he must learn to fight only for what is important, and not against people. He must assert himself inwardly and express himself with courage and discipline. Having become aware of the power of his personal ego as well as of the limitations that prevent his soul from expressing the best of himself, the candidate is ready for the crossing. He aspires now, as in *Invictus*[55], the poem that inspired Nelson Mandela, to become the captain of his soul.

THE CROSSING, TO BECOME THE CAPTAINS OF OUR SOULS

The Solidarity Being and the Opening of the Heart

This stage marks the discovery of the inner being, the space within oneself in which confidence reigns. And the doors of the heart are opened. *The Solidarity Being* is the person who opens his heart and becomes sensitive to the suffering of others. With tenderness, he attends to the wounds of others and develops compassion, gentleness and generosity. The practice of altruism becomes possible.

One of the first qualities that is awakened on the heroic

55 Poem by English writer William Ernest Henley that inspired Nelson Mandela during his twenty seven years in prison.

path is the quality of service; serving not because we are asked for something, but because we choose to put ourselves at the service of a cause that calls us, for people who are in need. The practice of compassion, that is to say, of feeling the difficulties and pain of others, goes hand in hand with the development of real respect for oneself and others, a great humanism that teaches us to take care of others, but also of ourselves. This stage teaches discernment and confidence without naivety, but one must always be careful of the danger of giving of ourselves while neglecting our own needs, which may lead to the feeling of being taken advantage of…

The shadow of *the Solidarity Being* is that of the martyr, the person who ensures and maintains his power over others by making them feel guilty, and by playing the savior, when in reality he keeps those he helps in a childish state, stifling them. The initial goal of the *Solidarity Being* is trust and openness, but he must be able to fight against selfishness by learning to give without self-immolation and by maintaining compassion, kindness and generosity.

The Adventurer: Being a Dolphin

My master explained to me, at one point during my journey, that an adventure can be crazy but the adventurer must be sane. The sense of adventure appears when the soul calls us towards the unknown, towards the mystery of life and one's own existence. We cannot ignore this call, which comes with the challenges of making our dreams come true. But to face it, one must keep one's mind and heart in the center of the self, else the force of adventure will carry us away with its centrifugal movement and make us leave the path of our destiny. Then we run the risk of regression, with its share of frustrations.

This is why it is essential at this stage to keep the soul centered, but without diminishing its power. Some, taken over by impulsiveness, burn themselves like fireflies and can stay with their injuries for life. In the middle of this path we all must take the turn that leads us in the right direction.

The Adventurer is intensively engaged in the quest and he seeks the treasure because he has a powerful desire to further the growth of his true identity. In deep pursuit of meaning, the person who dares to set off on the adventure strives to find the meaning of his life and to exceed limits and limitations. He desires something beyond himself, and he tries to find that which cannot be spoken of, which will reveal his qualities.

Only when we respond to this call our journey really begins. We engage intensively in expressing our true identity through the ups and downs of our lives. *The Adventurer* seeks the best of life and fears nothing, other than conformity. He may fear danger instinctively, but nevertheless he courageously confronts the dragons that appear on the way, for the path of the disciple reveals itself before his eyes. *The Adventurer* wants to embark on the path of the *Peaceful Warrior* in order to regain his true identity; he is a seeker of truth.

The individual dominated by the shadow of the *Adventurer* is a perfectionist, trying endlessly to live up to an unrealizable goal. He suffers from the illness of those who live only for their own improvement. He has a great difficulty getting involved and can become a detached consumer, living in his world, prone to all kinds of dependencies.

To summarize, the *Adventurer* seeks to acknowledge his deep self. He must learn to persevere on his journey and keep moving despite difficulties, without falling into conformism. If he overcomes the trial he will gain autonomy in the management of conflicts. Researchers Ian Stewart and Vann

Joines[56] proposed a table of inner attitudes using the world of fish as an example.

They described four attitudes: the carp, who always thinks he is in a worse shape than others, and the double carp, who thinks that neither he nor others are good. These two profiles have passive, victim-like natures. In the same basin we also find the shark that, like the bellicose warrior, thinks he is much better than everyone else and that he has all rights. He is a predator without a conscience. And finally, a little further off, we find the dolphin; a strange animal which can save crew members who fall into the water and guide boats to a good port. The dolphin type person has the attitude of the *Peaceful Warrior*; he has good self-esteem and values others. In my experience, when tested, a lot of carps tend to become... sharks!...although they may want to be dolphins.

Which Attitude?

56 Manuel d'analyse transactionnelle, Ian Stewart and Van Joines, Editions Dunod-Inter, 2005, chapter 12 : Positions de vie.

The Peaceful Warrior: The Power of Commitment

The archetype of the *Peaceful Warrior* is actually not the end of the hero's journey but only the starting point. The hero brings the crossing to an end. The learning is the resolution of the battle, with the acceptance of tests and trials. But life does not bring us just a single trial; as we complete one, new trials appear. The *Peaceful Warrior*'s position must be consolidated constantly in order to face these trials successfully.

This requires constant purification of oneself, on all planes: physical, psychological and mental. It also requires purifying ourselves from negativity and past suffering, but also maintaining the positive experience brought by the fight. Purity of the heart is an essential key to achieve this. It is the most precious good which the *Peaceful Warrior* must safeguard at all costs.

Any form of negativity will lead the warrior to corruption, sooner or later, and to the loss of his achievements. The *Peaceful Warrior* experiences the true power of love, which causes him to renounce false freedom, and to devote himself to true freedom, which is an offering and a commitment. The treasure that emerges from this encounter is the realization of the true Self. There we see the opening of the heart, to love, to engage without calculation, and to experience the force of giving.

In this stage we must root ourselves in our ability to touch the depth of our being, but also in weaving or building relationships with others. It is here that we share love with all who are on the path, with gratitude to our masters, and with a deep commitment. For now, the challenge of the *Peaceful Warrior* is to engage with life. The foundations of altruistic love are put in place.

The shadow of the *Peaceful Warrior* is the jealousy born of comparison and the need to be recognized. When the disciple is taken over by the shadow, he becomes possessive and envious, fixated on the object of his love, a seducer, a victim of his passions and attachments who uses love to conquer. He then weaves superficial relationships, which will in turn give rise to feelings of reciprocal betrayals.

To summarize, the shadow of the *Peaceful Warrior* is the greedy person, who does not want to pay for his actions, and always looks for someone else to take responsibility for paying in his stead. Greed was the worst crime among the ancient Egyptians; they said that the greedy being has no right to the grave. "The greedy man identifies himself with his possessions and desires, rather than with what he is. He refuses, behind a disproportionate ambition, to assume his own law of action, his place in the world. Not recognizing himself as he is, he is profoundly egocentric, so he cannot at any time assume the principle of universal solidarity."[57]

The purpose of this archetype is to defeat one's own dragon and to discover the inner treasure by remaining faithful to the heart, whatever the difficulty. Emerging victorious from this ordeal, we can then establish a deep connection, as a link in the long chain of peaceful warriors.

THE RETURN: THE MYSTERIES OF TRANSFORMATION

The Mystes: Destroyer Of Old Forms

All traditional societies celebrated the mysteries, which awaken souls of individuals within the framework of their communities. The mysteries[58] are trials and ceremonies that took place on the margins of social life, in secrecy. These institutions created scenarios and special effects that placed

57 *Maat and the actuality of Ancient Egypt,* Fernand Schwarz, Editions Noeme, Paris 1996, page 103.

58 The words mystery and mystique are derived from the same Greek root: *mustes* ("Initiate in the cult of mysteries", from "he who holds closed (his mouth and eyes)", from *muo*: to close).

the individual in a suitable ambience to pass these tests. Their purpose was to bring the mystical dimension into the candidate's heart, understood as the power that enables the expansion of the soul, bringing about sufficient altitude to connect with the candidate's spirit, which alone is capable of overcoming the ordeals.

While passing through the trials of the Mysteries, which were also representations of the myths, the *mystes* became an actor. He was preparing to experience initiation, a rite of passage during which the old personality symbolically dies, in order to be reborn in a new state. Historically this quest leads the seeker to achieve a state of consciousness that connects to the Being.

This stage initiates the destruction of old forms through trials, in order to attain inner freedom. The goal of the *Mystes* is to grow. But he is afraid of death without rebirth. He would like to create new forms at once, but first he has to encounter all the problems connected with past forms. They will have to be confronted, for the *Mystes* must learn to "let go" of the past in order for change to take place.

The one who is now a *peaceful warrior* must learn to grow inwards and face the trials he encounters, and this requires a renunciation of the old forms. He discovers himself in the trial, measuring himself before the obstacles, recognizing his shadows, fighting his dragons, and accepting himself as he is.

To advance, he will have to go beyond his limitations and suffering, and to really destroy the obstacles of the past. At this stage, it is a matter of recognizing one's own shadows and dragons, while destroying negative voices and criticism directed to others and to life. Everything that seemed indispensable before is now effaced by the initiation, and a transformation of consciousness takes place. In alchemy, this stage is referred to as the black work, which consists of going to the heart, to the bottom of the mine, in order to extract the metal that represents the spirit.

In synthesis, the shadow of the *Mystes* is self-destruction, the lack of self-esteem that drives the desperate to the destruction of others and to excesses of all kinds, instead of crossing the trial from above. The purpose of the archetype of the *Mystes* is the metamorphosis of the person who succeeded in overcoming the fear of destruction and annihilation, while learning detachment through the virtue of humility.

The Link: Being Oneself

The *Mystes* has passed through all the phases, from death to rebirth, and the phase of purification has been accomplished. Now, in the middle of the return journey, the phase of changes and transformations begins. This phase will lead the *Mystes* through a metamorphosis towards the emergence of his new form. It is about gradually finding the channels for expressing the inner man, both in oneself and in our choices and behavior in the world. The step of the *Link* brings us closer to our true self, and prepares us for the final stage of the journey, the return to the kingdom and the profound transformation of our life.

We discover our own law of action, the *Svadharma* of the Hindus. If every person's self-realization corresponds to the same journey, to the same path, each of us reaches our goal through different and complementary forms. Some realize themselves through transmission, becoming teachers, pedagogues. Others by taking care of the wellbeing of others, becoming nurses or doctors. Still others want to understand, becoming researchers, scientists, and philosophers. The realization of these forms expresses our innermost vocations. Traveling on the path of the archetypes makes it possible to recognize one's own profound vocation or law of action, and to realize it.

Contrary to what we may think, these are not several different paths. The Path is the same for all, for the trials that we must pass in order to know ourselves, to dominate and to transform ourselves, are the same. By traversing it we succeed in expressing the distinct forms of our being's vocation. The seeking disciple must avoid the trap of putting vocation at the service of the personal ego, whose aim is temporal success. It is in the service of the being that the vocation of the candidate must express itself. And the candidate must put himself at the service of the universal by connecting as a link to the chain of humanity.

This vocation is the expression of the inner human being, both within ourselves, and in our choices and behavior in the world. The inner human being does not aspire to possess, but only to know how to be.

The person who falls under the shadow of the *Link* is characterized by an obsession for change, he is a victim of such abundance and such an internal churning that he manages to put nothing into practice in spite of great momentary successes. He is a workaholic, in frantic action, and he abhors vacuum.

In summary, the purpose of the *Link* archetype is to become a channel for something that transcends one's personal ego, to learn to find meaning and one's true vocation and mission in life, while distrusting any lack of authenticity.

The Wisdom-Warrior

His aim is to participate in the construction of a prosperous and harmonious kingdom, where individuals can express Ma'at, as advocated by the ancient Egyptians, that is to say, metaphysical goods such as justice, solidarity and authenticity. His task is to help others find the meaning of their deep and true selves, while cultivating his own self. Here lies the necessity of gaining command over oneself, before governing others. For this, we must develop an internal power rather than seek authority for the power that comes with it.

To guide others means to place boundaries and rules that will help them grow through trials by expressing their innermost self. One may not feel up to the task, but the love for others, seeing their distress, and the need to elevate one's consciousness, are always motors for giving the best. In reality, every person already has what he needs, since in every person there is an incorruptible luminous diamond that expresses the best of oneself. What we need is to be shown the path that will lead us to extract our diamond consciousness from the well of inner shadows.

The shadow of the Wisdom-Warrior is the tyrant, the person who tries to control everything, flouting respect and dignity for others. In fables this is symbolized by the ogre. The tyrant insists excessively on his way of seeing things and annihilates the creativity of others. He gives orders without perceiving the consequences, and wants control at all costs…

To summarize, the purpose of this archetype is to connect with and to build what the Greeks called the *Kosmos* - an intelligent order, a wisdom of life. The Wisdom-Warrior assumes total responsibility for his life, awakening the inner power that protects us from failures and from the forces of chaos.

The Ascending Spiral

The heroic journey is an ascending spiral leading us to overcome our self-imposed limitations. At every end of a round in the spiral, if we are successful, another higher round awaits us, continuing the preceding one. Travelers on this path will know their true accomplishment only at their last breath. For this reason the Greeks never made statues of living human beings, which is a very good idea; they always waited for life's conclusion to decide if it fulfilled the conditions for heroization. The stages repeat themselves with each new cycle, but our consciousness is required to rise to a higher level.

While in the journey the stages are the same, the trials never repeat. They appear in deeper forms and in ways we would have never imagined. The difference in each new cycle is the experience, and the practice obtained in previous cycles. Everything becomes more subtle and refined, experiences are less emotional, and the mind achieves a more advantageous height.

There is a stronger perception of the invisible laws and in the face of action and trials regeneration is faster.

Many things that previously would have bothered us, and would have given our dark allies the opportunity to surface, cease to be important. We learn to celebrate life by learning to live the day to day. Confidence in the inner process increases even as we are faced with more powerful dragons, which are in fact an indication that we are making progress. Gradually, by overcoming trials, we build ourselves an inner structure that seats our deepest nature, a better and morally stronger force emerges to sustain our works.

CHAPTER VIII

The Warrior's Weapons

Love is the warrior's sword; wherever it strikes, it brings life, not death. Since time immemorial, the first thing warriors learned was to master a weapon. It was important to learn how to handle the weapon, whether it is a sword, a sling, a club, etc. In the inner combat, the weapons are perseverance, vigilance, temperance, courage and prudence. Inner weapons are moral qualities used in combat.

But this is not really the prevailing discourse, and it is not very well accepted as a mode of social action, which partly explains the huge lack of inner reference points. It is largely for this reason that our society has some difficulties today... the fear of saying things and assuming truths, and the lack of reference points to understand these truths. The result is that our present society disarms its citizens.

We need to learn to act from our center. If the center of our physical body is located at what the Orientals call the *hara*, a few centimeters below the navel, the energetic center is located at the solar *plexus* and the center of projection and perception lies in the middle of the forehead, between the eyes, because our true center is not physical. Bodily elements are forms which enable us to take action on other, more subtle planes. But our center lies elsewhere, in the highest part we can conceive within ourselves. And it is from this inner center that we must learn to handle the weapons of the peaceful warrior.

Inner Weapon no. 1: Mental Clarity

The path of the peaceful warrior begins with accepting our imperfections, with fighting our weaknesses with our bare hands. We cannot choke or hide our weaknesses without diminishing ourselves. The only option is to expose them, to take responsibility for them, so they become a force. Preparing the weapons of inner combat is done first by finding a clear vision; concentrating in order to launch the inner battle. It is imperative to put our thoughts in order, to calm down, so that the mind can once again play its role and discern, without our negative emotions acting as parasites.

Inner Weapon no. 2: Knowing How to Adapt, to Accept Contradictions

The art of inner mastery is based on being able to adapt to the changing course of things. We cannot predict exactly what will happen next. But if things do not happen the way we want them to, we get tense and stiffen up, and life ceases to flow. Tension is painful at the physical level and worse still at the emotional and mental level. Disappointment, anger, ill-being: who among us has never gone through these states? To know where to go, the best approach is to have clear intentions and just goals, without overly imagining how to reach the goal. To achieve this, we have to adapt to reality and to circumstances, which often do not depend solely on us. The path of the peaceful warrior is the art of adaptation, in which the peaceful warrior trains to preserve the flexibility of the mind. To adapt does not mean to submit, but to find adequate and intelligent forms of action with new inner means. Contrary to what is commonly believed, adaptability does not only serve the instinct of survival - which only seeks to preserve what has already been acquired - but also demonstrates the creative dimension of the human being.

Inner Weapon no. 3: To Know How to Climb

How should we fight that which makes us tense and stiff? By relaxing. And this fight is by far the most difficult. For it requires us to diminish the importance we give to what we want, and to what we are attached to, sometimes in an obsessive way. Learning to relax does not mean to soften up! When emotion takes over, our full attention is focused on it, and our consciousness is dragged down to the least brilliant dimension of ourselves. Our vision of reality is altered as in a distorting mirror.

For the peaceful warrior, such a situation is an excellent test of his combat skills. Who is going to prevail: the emotions or the burgeoning awareness? Before fighting anything, one must first be able to defeat oneself... This is a daily struggle, which takes place everywhere, down here where the laws of existence are realized. It is important to be able to lift yourself above yourself, to change your level of consciousness. Transcending one's existence is the true spiritual practice.

Inner Weapon no. 4: To Dare to Get Out of Ourselves

The real battle takes place in the field of our weaknesses. It is the struggle to "be" and not simply to exist. "Being" implies the actualization of a dormant potential, one that we need to invoke. We must dare to venture beyond ourselves, to risk giving the best of ourselves.

It is an inner battle. To refuse it is to confine ourselves to the fields we already conquered, mastered and know, where we think we can win effortlessly. Many people act this way and initially they do succeed, when on a well-chosen battlefield. But this is a one-time victory. Sooner or later, the heady question of meaning surfaces and it's impossible to address it. And then the infamous depression ensues, the mid-life crisis. It is born of having chosen the wrong battlefield, which is not really ours. We thought we could conquer our skills there, but we cannot conquer our deep qualities.

Inner Weapon no. 5: Retrieve Our Memory

Clarifying one's purpose and retrieving our memory is crucial. To be intelligent and capable of discernment, is not an intellectual ability. It requires us to see through things, to grasp what lies beyond appearances. To recover our intelligence, we must remember ourselves; we must know ourselves, and most importantly, recognize and remember where we came from, and who we really are. He who retrieves his memory will not go astray: it will become a guiding compass. Therefore he will not sink into anger, for he will know where to go.

The ancestral teachings of the *Bhagavad Gita* offer us a great opportunity: to retrieve the memory of our humanity. The peaceful warriors who preceded us have accomplished things that still lie dormant within us. These accomplishments resonate with our soul to this very day and open unsuspected channels.

Sometimes we find ourselves in the dark. And just as listening to a piece of music subtly changes our inner state, the message of the peaceful warriors, the example of their lives, can touch our barely awakened souls. The music penetrated the wall we had built between ourselves and the laws of the universe. It touched us directly, awoke us. But if we didn't already have within us that which the music awakened, it wouldn't have been able to do it, no matter how beautiful the music might have been. Great musicians touch us because they themselves have experienced something profound. The transmission of the path of the peaceful warrior works in the same way, which is why it still touches us today. If we want the warrior to be born, we must first retrieve our memory, the memory of the soul.

Without denying the value of an improved material existence, we must ensure that it does not cause internal impoverishment, such that people become trapped in their habits, unable to challenge themselves and change. Material wellbeing should no longer be used to mask or compensate for internal poverty. If we do not want our inner being to die, let us preserve our intelligence, let us retain our faculty of discernment. Let us develop our memory to improve our knowledge of where we have come from, because without memory, there would be no identity that could retain our experiences. We will therefore lose our very identity.

Any person that does not know who he really is, will not use his intelligence correctly. To keep our memory intact, we must let go of anger, because anger makes us forget who we are. Let us learn to put less emphasis on having and more on being.

In summary, we can say that the peaceful warrior is a person who uses discernment correctly, protects his memory and fights anger and attachment to things.

CHAPTER IX

The Inner Rules

The secret of happiness does not lie in the constant pursuit of more, but in being grateful with less.

Rule no. 1: The Battle is Natural for the Warrior

The peaceful warrior's battle is to face the mysteries of existence, the transformative trials, which he will have to face, despite not knowing the outcome. The transformation, however, is only confirmed if we can develop a greater ability to act, otherwise we do not change.

But are we determined to mobilize ourselves to make this change?

During combat, things appear to slow down. We do not see them unfolding with their natural velocity. On a daily basis, it is up to us to not get caught up in the syndrome of external speed, which slows down the inner being. The peaceful warrior, in fact must accelerate outside and slow down inside; abandon superficiality, and go back to the center. If we are caught up with our senses, or our anxieties, we lose ourselves, we descend and disperse. Instead, if we accept an inward journey, we would see the same things but at a distance, because we will be centered. Our center, our interior, is the summit from which the peaceful warrior observes.

The secret of the warrior is not to seek more, but to become able to be grateful with less. We must simplify and accept that to defeat an enemy we need to learn to know ourselves and not to rush to the battlefield before being ready, while accepting the inner rules of conduct. The peaceful warrior must persevere, fight and respect the rules, for there is no form without rules. The first rule is to accept the discipline of life, to obey one's choices, and to respect them.

It's not as simple as it sounds. We make many choices, but because we are often motivated by desire, we want these choices to be realized immediately and to obtain everything without a long process, without waiting. It is not so easy to overcome impulsiveness, to maintain intention, and to develop it continuously. The authentic hero realizes that he is a child of Heaven and Earth, that he is in between. This is true for all of us, but we sometimes refuse to become the bridge, a channel between Heaven and Earth.

In Heaven we will find a lot of inspiration and strength, and on Earth an infinite number of means to realize them. We cannot choose one over the other. Dual consciousness is necessary, that of being both a temporal being and a spiritual being. By learning to live these two natures at once, the heroic nature becomes more natural. Stay stable. Circumstances will always offer us battles, there's no need to look for them. Problems arrive by themselves, and when we want to advance, there is always an obstacle, a person, a critic... or many of these. These teachings remind us that other peaceful warriors have already passed through this very point, have experienced this path before us, and have advanced, left signs and continued to transmit the legacy of the soul, of how to become a peaceful warrior.

Rule no. 2: Lose the Victim Attitude

Mediocrity drives us to always find fault in others, but in reality what happens to us is directly or indirectly the consequence of our own actions. This is what eastern traditions call *karma*, the law of cause and effect. When pusillanimity triumphs, the warrior gives in and no longer seeks to conquer. He tries just to survive, to run away - because he sees himself as a victim. This is the worst attitude to approach a battle with. A victim can turn into a hangman. A tormentor can then imagine himself a victim. It is an intolerable, terrible dialectic that we are forced to experience in the 21st century. The world of tormentors and victims.

This attitude robs us of our heroic vision. A person who has a small image of himself is afraid of everything, and will try to survive just for the sake of self-preservation. The more you think little of yourself, the more you lose courage and cease to mobilize the will. At that point it becomes impossible to prevail, and softness, inertia and automatism are instilled. We must not think little of ourselves; but simply acknowledge our smallness – which is very different.

Unlike other living beings on the planet, humans are able to imagine themselves differently than they presently are. We can see ourselves as we are – and the path of the peaceful warrior can help us - but at the same time we can also imagine ourselves differently, and begin the process of becoming that other. But if the pettiness of the mind imprisons us, it is over. Everything then is but a moment of reverie, a sort of illusion…

"It is poorness of spirit [pusillanimity] that has smitten away from me my (true heroic) nature, my whole consciousness is bewildered in its view of right and wrong."[59]

With this sentence, Arjuna realizes the course of the

59 The Bhagavad Gita. Translated by Sri Aurobindo. Chapter II, Verse 7

peaceful warrior, which consists of defying softness, letting go of comfort, overcoming inertia and setting oneself in motion. The inner battle takes place every day and at every moment. It requires self-regeneration, in everything we do. This means that you must love what you do, and why you do it, otherwise it is impossible. This is why love is so important, because it holds the energy of liberation that can bring about regeneration. Finally, everything is played out at the same time: the opening of our hearts and the opening of our minds, in order to regain our courage and our heroic vision. Let us therefore leave behind pusillanimity and this terrible attitude which binds us to think about the details, while being unable to see the whole picture.

We are not victims of life, or of anyone. Whatever happens to us, we bring on ourselves, for better or worse. Circumstances, like the people around us, are elements that put us to the test and enable us to learn from life. We can succeed and prevail, or fail. And if we fail, we will have to learn from our failure. For the warrior, pain is a call to attention, to awareness, an expression of the body, or of something else.

Rule no. 3: Error is the Great Master

Anyone who claims to follow the path of the peaceful warrior must begin simply - take courage by the hand and act. We will make many mistakes. The great Master's name is "Error". He is very powerful, and we cannot move forward, if we do not listen to him. On the other hand, if we learn from experience, even if we do not like it, we will be able to learn and progress. We learn from our mistakes, get up and move forward. It is vain to try and show we already understood and know everything, and that we are not going to make any mistake. Such a person will be afraid of deceiving himself and will either not take action at all, or will take refuge in things he already knows to do. Trying to be perfect, or to be up to the task, we sometimes stop. We must learn from action. Errors are natural. What is not natural is to refuse to face them.

Rule no. 4: Transforming Anger into Action, Not Resentment

Anger has the peculiar ability to make us lose control of ourselves. This is the worst thing that can happen to us. By breaking the link that connects us to the center, we become vulnerable to our weaknesses. If we want to channel our energy, and not to poison ourselves from within, we must take action.

We should take action that soothes us: walking or pumping weights - an action that tires us physically. This physical fatigue will help us calm the mind and elevate it. In fact, when our mind resists life as it is, it feels tensions resulting from emotions we interpret as fear, sadness, anger.

The true emotions of the peaceful warrior are lasting sentiments, such as love, beauty, goodness and righteousness, which are connected with the perennial dimension of reality. They are related to that something within us that we can count on, and on which others can also rely.

This is something simple and profoundly heroic.

In the Hindu tradition as in the Platonic tradition, the warrior's field of action is the plane of emotions and sentiments, which is called *linga* in Sanskrit. This word is the source of the term *lingam*, which designates the generative organ of the God Shiva. Lingam is not simply a phallus, it is the organ of begetting, the virile and fecundating source, the perpetual basis of the re-creation of the world and of each one of us. And the god Shiva is none other than the great dancer, who produces the rhythms of the world, the warrior god who dances for death, and with his movements engenders life.

In Greece this power is associated with Dionysus and in Egypt with Osiris. The important thing, however, is the association of the path of the peaceful warrior with *linga*, that is to say, with the capacity to erect, through self-restraint and concentration, an emerging, creative and powerful column to illuminate the world.

The path of the peaceful warrior must be oriented towards the transformation of emotions into actions, inspired by lasting sentiments, notably those of honor and loyalty.

Rule no. 5: Control and Replace Habits with Voluntary Attention

In the path of the peaceful warrior, no passivity or automatism is possible. That is why we speak of being "conscious". All evolution and improvement requires attention. Being new, it is a mystery that asks us to be present, to exercise our voluntary attention.

Voluntary attention enables us to know where we are and who we are. Any encounter with others can then become a generous gift of presence wherein we can give without losing ourselves. If we want to be conscious, we must learn to increasingly develop our voluntary attention. For it is not people or circumstances that must awaken us; but it is us who want to be awake. In this way, we can never calculate what to expect, we must simply remain attentive, therefore conscious.

We have an important battle to win because our attention is limited and the state of our awareness can weaken. On the path of the peaceful warrior, everyday life becomes an exercise to remain conscious, to sustain attention for longer periods. Involuntary attention requires stimuli and external attractions which make us react. The inner battle, on the other hand, requires action from within; it cannot be a reaction. We should pay attention then to many more things than we are used to.

Habit is mechanical; it seeks comfort and makes us withdraw our attention, our presence and our open mind. Everything seems easier, but in the long run we lack points of reference and become confused.

Only the practice of voluntary attention allows us to prevail, but it requires us to develop courage and vigilance. It is impossible to cross boundaries, without overcoming our fears or remaining vigilant and attentive. Action requires consciousness, that is, presence. Many people can be at a certain place without really being there, they occupy a physical place but are not attentive, as if in a dream. They are there, but are not present. Vigilance means not to lose awareness, to "catch ourselves in the act" of distraction. Automatism is an unconscious search for comfort. The real pursuit of comfort is not driven by material goods, but in the refusal to think of, and take care of, others; to want to be left alone.

Rule no. 6: Daring to Go Into The Unknown

Staying on the path requires us to come to terms with the unknown. There exists a stranger within us, and we must meet him. The human being has evolved because he has embarked into the mystery of the unknown. The challenge of the unknown forces us to emerge from a comfortable place in order to mobilize our potential to create new means and new qualities. Every time we reject the unknown, in a way we regress.

Rule no. 7: Learning to Fall

Falling means to learn to land safely. If you learn to land, even if you fail, even if you are beaten, you will not be hurt, physically or morally, and your confidence will remain untouched. But if you do not know how to land, you will have serious problems. On the one hand you will have pain, while on the other, your confidence and courage will weaken. You will intellectualize many useless things and fail.

The first philosophy to learn is to land safely, so that you learn to know yourself and to recognize yourself; using the same forces you used to land and to recover. Falling is an art; the more we are tense, the more we are hurt.

We have to follow through with movement, because we cannot stop it; it is therefore a matter of following through and relaxing.

Breathing is essential, but we do not know how to breathe. One must learn to breathe in order to calm the heart. When we are agitated, the heart beats too fast. We must learn to make it beat slower and to reduce our respiratory movements by filling the lungs well.

To accept ourselves is fundamental in order to land safely and requires us to accept our failures without ignoring our weaknesses. Our weaknesses and difficulties must simply make us aware of what we need to change. Managing our pain, not to complain but to understand, is essential to change. One cannot evolve nor change without having the right starting point - which is our weaknesses and not our assets!

Rule no. 8: Move into Action!

The important thing is not the result of the battle, but the process of the battle itself, that is, our ability to follow the rules, to maintain a good inner state, and be able to respond to difficulties. The important thing on the path of the peaceful warrior is to not worry, so as to be able to remain calm in the face of difficulties. Whether or not there will be results, is not always in our control. But what does depend on us is to remain focused and calm, and to continue, because on this path we are entitled to only one thing: action.

Without action, one cannot learn. We must first decide to simply act. It is simpler than we imagine because any true, deep, philosophy is simple and can be taught by example and not only with words. This means we can only transmit what we have managed to live intensely and understand ourselves. And if we have not lived it, we need to recognize that we do not know how to do it, recognize what we have not yet achieved, recognize what we do not know - that will be our first wise act!

Rule no. 9: Patience

The process of cultivating the peaceful warrior requires the practice of patience. In the Voice of the Silence it is said: "Remember, thou that fightest for man's liberation, each failure is success (because you will learn from it), and each sincere attempt wins its reward in time."

We must accept that the path is gradual and long. We must learn patience. Patience is not just waiting; it is a form of action. Do not imagine patience as a stop. In India, patience is called *Shanti* and it is one of the six essential disciplines to practice, because only patience allows us to experience the process. In Indian philosophy, *Shanti* is our capacity to create additional space within, so things can enter.

Through patience, we can have confidence that something, eventually, will become an integral part of ourselves, although it is not yet. As we have not yet become what we want to be, it is good to have confidence in something we are yet to be, but would like to become, or think we can become.

If things are in this space within, they become part of us, and can accompany us every day. When we wake up, when we go to bed, when we eat, they are always with us. This inner space allows us to integrate these realities for which we know we have to be patient, giving them room to grow and to develop.

It is a long and inexorable evolutionary process to gain confidence in our capacity to evolve, to realize that we have a potential within that deserves to be activated. In practice, we need to integrate the thing we wish for into our inner space. Just like the seed is received by the earth to be nurtured patiently, what we wish and want with patience will grow and take root. It is a matter of having the goals we want to achieve as a permanent companion in our life, in our feelings and thoughts. This doesn't mean to relegate things, but rather to give them a lot of attention. Because while things are embryonic, they are very frail, like an embryo still inside its mother's womb. They must be fed, and be constantly attended to.

Irritation and impatience arise when the things we want are not within our space...

Patience comes from trust: confidence in the plant that has just been planted, confidence in the education given to the child, in the teachings transmitted to the disciples, so that one day they may be able to profit by it. When we lack confidence impatience appears. Without a patient attitude, it is useless to begin. If we wish to evolve, we will have to choose the camp of patience anyway... always knowing that in any case we will lose patience. That is the paradox of the path, but it is not a problem, because we will learn to be patient again!

CHAPTER X

The Adventure of Perseus

To Begin, a Myth

The heroic path allows us to fulfill our potential, but also enables us to become part of a clan, to integrate into a group, which, as sociologist Frederic Vincent[60] affirms, is something that lies beyond the individual self. In France and in many Western countries, isolation and loneliness are often the price paid for individualism.

"But if we look at the models that are presented to us in culture, films or television, for example, individualism is not highly valued. Ideally, it is a return to the community or tribe. One can only be a hero within a group, a community, a whole."[61]

In recent years, the figure of the ordinary hero has resurfaced, as is the case of the two soldiers of Thalys, or the civilian in Nice on July 14, 2016, who tried to slow down the truck driver on his suicide mission. But, there are also many

---

60 Frederic Vincent: http://fredericvincent.fr/

61 *Psychology of the Ordinary Hero* (Psychologie du héros ordinaire), Fréderic Vincent, Psychologie Magazine, May 2016.

anonymous people who, in floods or natural disasters, help their neighbors. These everyday heroes, born of "ordinary" people, prove that every person can surpass himself.

Inspired by these models I thought to present here what was transmitted to me and that I transmitted to others, about the ancient path of the peaceful warrior. To give a new meaning, another opportunity to the quest pursued by youth. They need not only an adventure, but also to express their inner altruism. When they do so, their souls become upright, and can give a transcendent meaning to their lives, making themselves available to the community.

A strange alchemy, between adventure and altruism, is necessary in order to bring out the daily hero which lies at the heart of every individual. What better way than an adventure, coupled with the desire to save lives? Thus, a few years ago, the Kraken weekends were born, a time for confrontation but also for competence training. But before continuing, here is the inspiring myth.

The Myth of Perseus

Perseus, whose name is derived from the Indo-European root *bher*, "to cut", was a prince of Argos. His mother, Danae, the daughter of King Acrisius, was locked up in a tower with brazen doors, guarded by ferocious dogs, for an oracle had predicted that she would bear a son who would one day kill his grandfather. *The oracle highlights a heroic destiny.*

Zeus, observing Danae from Olympus and seduced by her beauty, enters her room one day in the form of golden rain and gives her a son, Perseus. This child, son of heaven and earth, will be born in secret.

The golden rain is the call of being that one can hear, despite the obstacles posed by our egoism.

Perseus, betrayed by his cries, is locked into a chest with his mother and thrown into the sea. Destiny brings them to the island of Seriphos, where they are found by a generous fisherman, Dictys (the net), who takes charge of them and educates Perseus.

Like any other hero, Perseus is exiled. This is the beginning of any initiatic journey.

Time passes. An experienced seaman, accustomed to facing the raging waves, Perseus becomes a young man full of strength and audacity. The sovereign of Sériphos, Polydectes, one day notices the beauty of his mother Danae and despite her refusal, plans to marry her. At the banquet, a quarrel breaks out. Carried away by his impetuosity, Perseus makes a foolish deal with the rustic Polydectes: if he succeeds in bringing back the head of the terrifying Medusa - a monster with the body of a woman and the hair of serpents who turns into stone anyone who looks into her eyes - Polydectes would forgo the marriage with Danae. The King of Seriphos accepts his word, seeing it as an opportunity to eliminate once and for all the protector of the woman on whom he had set his sight.

This rash challenge shows Perseus as an idealist, outraged by injustice.

When Perseus becomes aware of the insurmountable challenge he has accepted, doubt overwhelms him. His divine origin at that moment plays in his favor. The gods Hermes and Athena, messengers of Zeus, bring him help through gifts and advice. From Hermes, Perseus receives a very sharp curved sword and a magic bag into which an object of any size can enter. Athena gives him a shield with a surface so perfectly polished that it reflects light as a mirror. Thanks to the Nymphs of the Styx, he also finds Hades' hat of invisibility and winged sandals like those of Hermes.

Hermes and Athena are the masters of wisdom who guide our steps. The gifts they present to Perseus are our latent potentialities. It is up to us to make them operational.

Hermes tells Perseus how to find Medusa's lair: he must go to the Graeae, sisters of the Gorgons, in the land of shadows, so that they may reveal to him the way, which they alone know. The Graeae are three swan-bodied women who were old even before they were born; they are called *Dino* the frightening, *Enyo* the bellicose and *Pemphredo* the wicked.

The Graeae represent the shadows in each of us, our vices, our prejudices that prevent us from advancing, transforming ourselves, to become better. To think that one has seen everything, that one has nothing more to learn, is true old age.

At the end of a long journey, Perseus arrives at the den of the Graeae. They try to manipulate him, to make him give up his mission. But Perseus is cleverer than they are; to get what he wants, he steals the only eye and the only tooth they have, which they share to see and feed.

Shadows, deprived of sight and the ability to bite, can no longer subdue the hero.

Perseus now knows the way he must take to meet his enemy. He heads westward to the land of the Hyperboreans, until he reaches her home. Hundreds of petrified stone-men with disfigured faces lie in the long underground corridors where the monster resides.

Thanks to Athena's mirror shield, Perseus is able to approach the Gorgon without being petrified by her gaze. His own reflection allows him to guide his movement and to cut her head which is bristling with snakes.

The mirror symbolizes consciousness. In this mirror, Perseus sees himself in action. He can observe himself, correct himself and defeat Medusa - his fear.

Perseus gathers the head of Medusa and puts it in his magic bag. From the blood of the monster, a winged horse arises, called Pegasus. Perseus tames and rides him back to his country.

Pegasus, like the phoenix, symbolizes rebirth. The hero who has defeated his fears reaches a new dimension of being and can take flight.

On the way back, Perseus flies over the Phoenician coast. There, a drama is taking place: Princess Andromeda is to be sacrificed to the *Kraken*, a terrifying sea monster that threatens to ravage everything. Perseus falls in love with Andromeda and decides to help her. Using the petrifying power of the head of Medusa, he manages to defeat the *Kraken*.

The Kraken represents all the devastating passions that prevent humanity from becoming realized. The city is ready to sacrifice its princess - its soul! - so as not to have to face the consequences of its actions. The peaceful warrior who has assumed the inner battle can put himself at the service of others, and become a civilizing hero by restoring justice to the heart of the city.

Perseus and Andromeda arrive at Seriphos. They discover that Danae and Dictys have taken refuge in a temple to flee the wrath of King Polydectes, who wanted to force Perseus's mother to marry him. Perseus shows Medusa's head to the king and his followers and they turn to stone. He then entrusts the throne of Sériphos to Dictys and leaves for Argos. On the way, the prophecy is fulfilled and Perseus accidentally kills his grandfather. Considering himself unworthy of ruling over Argos, he exchanges his kingdom with the king of Tiryns and becomes a very good ruler. Athena then asks Perseus to return the magic objects, and she keeps the shield, fixing the head of the Gorgon on it.

The return to Seriphos symbolizes the return of the hero, which brings his journey to an end. He incarnates the archetype of the judge and the ruler as a warrior of wisdom *and restores to the gods the magical tools that have helped him in his crossing, since they are now within him.*

After his death, Athena creates a place for him in the heavens, amongst the constellations, accompanied by Andromeda, the sea monster Kraken, Cepeus and Cassiopeia.

After his death the hero is deified and rejoins the origins, the celestial world, in order to guide, with the stars, souls on their earthly journey.

Perseus: The Journey of the Peaceful Warrior

To transform myth into history, one must pass through the phase of action. The Kraken outings in New Acropolis (France) aim to defeat our dragons, our inner kraken. After a few exercises and trials that build solidarity within the group, we gather around a fire with a 'speaker's staff', as in ancient times, and each one in turn is asked to speak about their own inner battle.

Then, several humanitarian, social and environmental volunteering projects are initiated, in which the rules of the peaceful warrior are applied. Gradually, thanks to the qualifications of my team-mates, several participants are trained in different techniques on a semi-professional level. They have become citizens who, by their example and experience, are able to bring positive elements to the society and community to which they belong.

The soul of France inspires them in all its various facets

and archetypes; sometimes it is nourishing, sometimes it is mystical, and sometimes warlike or political.

This is a path of hope. Abdennour Bidar[62] accurately points out what has already been evident for a few decades: all our contemporary crises are crises of bonding - bonding with our inner being, with humanity, with nature.

The Greeks had already proposed the three essential links we need to reestablish. First, the link with ourselves, which leads us to discover our deeper self and listen to it as well as to realize our highest aspirations with dignity, without feeling obliged to do the same as everybody else. Then there is the bond with others, to live together, to flourish through the practice of solidarity and altruism, without ulterior motives. And finally, the link with nature and the universe, for which we must regain the respect due to the sources of life that our action relies on. This also enables us to understand the importance of harmonizing with the laws of life in order to build a civilization that honors not only the human being, but life itself.

All these ties are genuine resources that can regenerate, inspire and comfort us at any point in our lives. They are the source of enthusiasm and they are creative forces, since they enable us to bring out the best of ourselves at every moment and share it with others.

The journey of the peaceful warrior was designed to reestablish these links and to recreate a womb that allows rebirth. Born again, we can see that life is worth living and that dreams can become reality. As the ancient Egyptians explained, in our heart-consciousness are woven the bonds that broaden consciousness and vision. It is up to us to seize

---

62 According to the article *They Already Weave the Future* published in the newspaper Le Monde, August 20, 2016.

the opportunity to walk this path of hope and victory.

Believe in Youth

"The French youth cannot be reduced to the nihilism of the jihadists. Let us not shatter their hopes. It is up to us to allow teens to invent the future."[63]

Civilizations die when transmission between generations ceases. Generations lacking reference points have succeeded each other since May 1968. The transmission of essential values has been diluted by the mentality of consensus and consumption, where appearances are given priority. Therefore, we find ourselves unable to listen to the vocation of our children, and they obtain diplomas that simply allow them to find work and social recognition.

But younger generations are less attracted by these sirens and want authentic and consistent narratives. They do not want to copy their elders, and instead can listen and understand, when the messages reflect their real life experience. Playing a role with the youth is possible, necessary and important, but it requires us to be able to inspire their souls and awaken their self-confidence, without trying to impose any model upon them.

It is by believing in them and helping them unveil their own potential that we will make them discover their own freedom of destiny. As the English psychoanalyst pediatrician Donald Winnicott said, they must be allowed to think again "that life is worth living" for itself, for oneself and for others. But also to make them understand that they can build a new world and above all, one that is better than ours. Better, not in a technological or economic sense, but more human, capable of more solidarity and of achieving the common good; a world in which everyone would find their right place. The path of

63 Croire en nos enfants, Article by Marie-Rose Moro, Le Monde, 17 August 2016.

the peaceful hero seems to be one of the operative proposals for successful transmission and the awakening of youth.

Nelson Mandela said: "I always knew that in the depths of every human being there were compassion and generosity ... People must learn to hate, and if they can learn to hate, they can also learn to love because love comes more naturally to a human heart than its opposite ... Goodness is a flame that can be hidden but never extinguished."

Gandhi similarly said, "Be the change you want to see in the world."

In order to regain a spirituality capable of changing the world, we must first return to ourselves and transform ourselves.

NEW ACROPOLIS
INTERNATIONAL ORGANIZATION

International Organization New Acropolis

New Acropolis is a worldwide non-profit organization, with centres in over fifty countries.

Established by Professor Jorge Angel Livraga on the foundations of practical philosophy and universal fraternity, New Acropolis is inspired by a fundamental respect for human dignity beyond differences of race, gender, culture, religion or socio-economic status. New Acropolis respects diversity but also tries to transcend it in search of a higher unity through shared universal ethical principles.

At New Acropolis, philosophy is more than just intellectual food for thought. We study philosophy as a means to integrate science, arts, ethics and metaphysics in order to work towards global human development.

This vision is implemented through a wide range of programs that combine practical education with cultural and volunteering activities. New Acropolis also promotes an awareness of current affairs, both locally and globally and focuses on improving the human condition by aligning ourselves with the laws of nature.

To learn more about New Acropolis, visit www.acropolis.org